GLOBALVIEWPOINTS

Cybercrime

Other Books of Related Interest:

At Issue Series

Cyberpredators

Policing the Internet

What Is the Impact of Twitter?

Global Viewpoints Series

Social Networking

Opposing Viewpoints Series

Cybercrime

Hacking and Hackers

GLOBALVIEWPOINTS

Cybercrime

Noah Berlatsky, Book Editor

GREENHAVEN PRESS
A part of Gale, Cengage Learning

GALE
CENGAGE Learning®

Detroit • New York • San Francisco • New Haven, Conn • Waterville, Maine • London

Elizabeth Des Chenes, *Director, Content Strategy*
Cynthia Sanner, *Publisher*
Douglas Dentino, *Manager, New Product*

For more information, contact:
Greenhaven Press
27500 Drake Rd.
Farmington Hills, MI 48331-3535
Or you can visit our Internet site at gale.cengage.com

Articles in Greenhaven Press anthologies are often edited for length to meet page requirements. In addition, original titles of these works are changed to clearly present the main thesis and to explicitly indicate the author's opinion. Every effort is made to ensure that Greenhaven Press accurately reflects the original intent of the authors. Every effort has been made to trace the owners of copyrighted material.

Cover image © Ann Cutting/Workbook.

LIBRARY OF CONGRESS CATALOGING-IN-PUBLICATION DATA

Cybercrime / Noah Berlatsky, book editor.
    p. cm. -- (Global viewpoints)
    Includes bibliographical references and index.
    ISBN 978-0-7377-6906-7 (hardcover) -- ISBN 978-0-7377-6907-4 (pbk.)
    1. Computer crimes. I. Berlatsky, Noah, editor of compilation.
    HV6773.C918 2013
    364.16'8--dc23
                                                                    2013001173

Printed in the United States of America
    1 2 3 4 5   17 16 15 14 13

Contents

Chapter 2: Law and Cybercrime

Chapter 4: Cyber Espionage and Cyberterrorism

Foreword

Global interdependence has become an undeniable reality. Mass media and technology have increased worldwide access to information and created a society of global citizens. Understanding and navigating this global community is a challenge, requiring a high degree of information literacy and a new level of learning sophistication.

Building on the success of its flagship series, Opposing Viewpoints, Greenhaven Press has created the Global Viewpoints series to examine a broad range of current, often controversial topics of worldwide importance from a variety of international perspectives. Providing students and other readers with the information they need to explore global connections and think critically about worldwide implications, each Global Viewpoints volume offers a panoramic view of a topic of widespread significance.

Drugs, famine, immigration—a broad, international treatment is essential to do justice to social, environmental, health, and political issues such as these. Junior high, high school, and early college students, as well as general readers, can all use Global Viewpoints anthologies to discern the complexities relating to each issue. Readers will be able to examine unique national perspectives while, at the same time, appreciating the interconnectedness that global priorities bring to all nations and cultures.

Material in each volume is selected from a diverse range of sources, including journals, magazines, newspapers, nonfiction books, speeches, government documents, pamphlets, organization newsletters, and position papers. Global Viewpoints is truly global, with material drawn primarily from international sources available in English and secondarily from US sources with extensive international coverage.

Features of each volume in the Global Viewpoints series include:

- An **annotated table of contents** that provides a brief summary of each essay in the volume, including the name of the country or area covered in the essay.

- An **introduction** specific to the volume topic.

- A **world map** to help readers locate the countries or areas covered in the essays.

- For each viewpoint, an **introduction** that contains notes about the author and source of the viewpoint explains why material from the specific country is being presented, summarizes the main points of the viewpoint, and offers three **guided reading questions** to aid in understanding and comprehension.

- **For further discussion** questions that promote critical thinking by asking the reader to compare and contrast aspects of the viewpoints or draw conclusions about perspectives and arguments.

- A worldwide list of **organizations to contact** for readers seeking additional information.

- A **periodical bibliography** for each chapter and a **bibliography of books** on the volume topic to aid in further research.

- A comprehensive **subject index** to offer access to people, places, events, and subjects cited in the text, with the countries covered in the viewpoints highlighted.

Global Viewpoints is designed for a broad spectrum of readers who want to learn more about current events, history, political science, government, international relations, economics, environmental science, world cultures, and sociology—students doing research for class assignments or debates, teachers and faculty seeking to supplement course materials, and others wanting to understand current issues better. By presenting how people in various countries perceive the root causes, current consequences, and proposed solutions to worldwide challenges, Global Viewpoints volumes offer readers opportunities to enhance their global awareness and their knowledge of cultures worldwide.

Introduction

"White supremacy has entered the digital era. Avowed white supremacist extremists, such as David Duke, . . . were early adopters of digital-media technologies. They were among the first to create, publish, and maintain web pages on the Internet."

—Jessie Daniels,
Cyber Racism: White Supremacy
Online and the New Attack on
Civil Rights. *Lanham, MD:
Rowman & Littlefield, 2009, p. 3*

One of the most controversial kinds of cybercrime is the use of the Internet to spread hate speech. Hate speech is intended to "intimidate, harm, or terrify not only a person, but an entire group of people to which the victim belongs," according to a June 15, 2011, article on the Canadian CBC News website. In Canada, as in many European countries, inciting hatred against a particular group—such as blacks, Jews, Muslims, homosexuals, or women—can be a crime. In particular, in Canada, spreading hatred through telecommunications equipment such as the Internet may be a crime and can be prosecuted as such. In its response to frequently asked questions, the website Partners Against Hate notes that besides Canada, the countries of Denmark, France, Britain, and Germany have all prosecuted individuals for spreading hate speech over the Internet. Moreover, the Council of Europe's Convention on Cybercrime—the first international treaty intended to harmonize national laws on cybercrime—includes hate crime provisions.

Those who support criminalizing hate crimes argue that the spreading of hate online leads "to crime in real life," as the

International Network Against CyberHate (INACH) argues in a June 2004 publication, "Hate on the Net: Virtual Nursery for In Real Life Crime." INACH goes on to argue that the Internet is frequently used by neo-Nazi groups to incite and encourage hatred and crimes against minorities. For instance, INACH points to the group National Rebirth of Poland (NOP), a group sponsored by Italian terrorists linked to a 1980 railway station attack that left eighty dead. INACH says that NOP uses its website to promote anti-Semitism, to publicize its paramilitary training camps, and to "encourage its followers to 'act' against 'enemies of the nation.'" INACH says that Poland's constitutional provisions against hate speech should in theory allow the government to close down hate sites. In practice, however, these provisions are poorly enforced.

Similarly, in a May 4, 2012, interview on Arutz Sheva, an Israeli news network, Ronald Eissens of the Magenta Foundation similarly argues that hate speech, especially anti-Semitism and Holocaust denial, should be removed from Internet sites such as Facebook, Twitter, and YouTube. Eissens points out that it is generally easier to push for the removal of hate crime speech in Europe than in the United States. For example, he says, Twitter is based in the United States and so has been reluctant to remove offensive material. Eissens adds that, as a result, "The number of anti-Semitic postings and those about Holocaust denial on Twitter are fairly high." He hopes, however, that as Twitter opens regional offices outside the United States, it will become more receptive to calls to remove hate speech.

But while Eissens hopes for broader application of hate crimes laws, other commentators have argued that hate crime laws are unjust and cannot be fairly implemented. Thomas Landen, in a January 28, 2009, article for the *Brussels Journal*, maintains that hate crime laws make justice subjective. "It is possible to objectively prove that someone has kidnapped, tortured and subsequently assassinated a victim, but is it also possible to prove that these acts constitute a worse crime if the perpetrator hates the victim . . .?" He adds that "hate speech, racial slurs, or insults directed against a majority group do not seem to be as equally punishable under hate crimes legislation as those directed against minorities." He says the result is that citizens in Europe "are no longer equal under the law."

While Landen worries that majority groups may not receive the same protection as minorities, others have suggested that, in fact, hate crime laws may result in discrimination against Muslims. In a February 8, 2006, article in the *Christian Science Monitor*, Mark Rice-Oxley reports that many Muslims feel that their religion is not afforded the same protection as Judaism. They argue that anti-Semitism is illegal and vigorously prosecuted in European nations. On the other hand, they say, anti-Muslim statements or images—such as a series of anti-Muslim cartoons that appeared in a Denmark newspaper—are tolerated. Rice-Oxley quotes Inayat Bunglawala of the Muslim Council of Britain, who stated, "Most of Europe would not dare mock the Holocaust, and rightly so." Bunglawala added, "Newspaper editors exercise good judgment every day when it comes to printing materials so as not to cause offense, so why not on this occasion?"

The United States has a First Amendment guarantee of free speech, and many have argued that hate crime laws in America are therefore unconstitutional. Nonetheless, some jurisdictions have passed hate crime laws, and they have been used to prosecute online speech. One notable case occurred in New Jersey, where Dharun Ravi, a student at Rutgers University, used a webcam to record his roommate, Tyler Clementi, engaging in a homosexual encounter with another male student. Clementi subsequently killed himself, and Ravi was convicted of invasion of privacy. In addition, however, he faced an even harsher jail sentence for a hate crime under New Jersey law. Eventually, Ravi received only thirty days in jail rather than the ten years possible under the hate crimes law. Nonetheless, Emily Bazelon, writing in a March 18, 2012, article for the *New York Times*, argues that "states like New Jersey and Massachusetts should narrow their civil rights laws" so that "young people . . . [do not] pay a too-heavy price for our fears about how kids use technology to be cruel."

Cyber hate is one of the most disputed types of criminal activity online, but it is far from the only form of cybercrime. The remainder of this book examines other kinds of illegal online activities and the laws that target such activities, in chapters titled Vulnerability to Cybercrime, Law and Cybercrime, Organized Crime and Cybercrime, and Cyber Espionage and Cyberterrorism. Different writers from around the world present different viewpoints about how to deal with the complex and changing issues surrounding cybercrime.

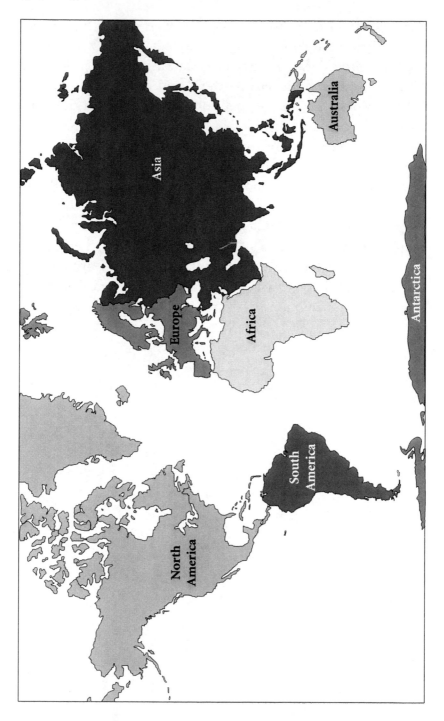

 **GLOBAL**VIEWPOINTS

Vulnerability to Cybercrime

Increased Internet Access in South Africa Makes It More Vulnerable to Cybercrime

Charles Goredema

Charles Goredema is a senior research fellow at the Institute for Security Studies (ISS) in South Africa. In the following viewpoint, he argues that the risks of cybercrime are growing in South Africa. This is in large part because of the growth of Internet and mobile phone use in the country. He says that the speed of Internet connections, the use of unprotected computer devices, and the use of data storage cards are particular causes of risk in South Africa. Goredema says that the public needs to be better informed and that more research needs to be done regarding forms and trends of cybercrime.

As you read, consider the following questions:

1. According to Goredema, what is the general consensus as to the definition of cybercrime?
2. What are data storage cards, and how does Goredema say they are vulnerable to cybercrime?
3. What legislation does Goredema say that South Africa has passed to combat cybercrime?

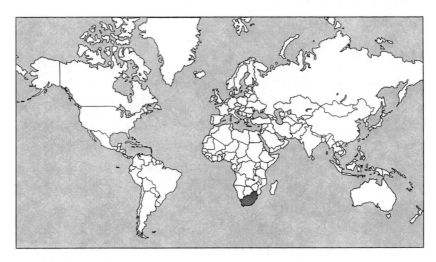

Nearly a year ago, a specialist in software risk management and data storage, Marthinus Engelbrecht, warned that while statistics on violent crimes in South Africa hit the head-lines every day because of their severity, cyber crimes were much more common and had a much bigger impact. Crime analysts and commentators have regularly warned about the insidious nature of cyber crime, and, occasionally predicted an upswing in its occurrence. The build up to the World Cup soccer tournament in 2010 [in South Africa], for example, provided a platform for estimates of scale, some of which appeared exaggerated. There are in fact no statistics to reflect what was eventually experienced. However, numerous factors indicate that the risk of South Africans falling victim to cyber crime has grown immensely.

The Intrusive Abuse of Computers

There is general consensus that cyber crime is any crime that is committed by means of a computer device which is linked to other computers through the Internet. At the same time, there is much uncertainty about the full range of such crimes and how they affect our daily lives. In a typical cyber crime situation, the computer may be used either as an instrument by which to initiate the crime, or as the target of the crime, as stated by the Council for Scientific and Industrial Research's Joey Jansen van Vuuren and Marthie Grobler in a study done in 2009. The scope of activities which could fall within the definition of cyber crime is potentially quite broad, ranging from purely malicious or intimidatory invasions of privacy, to the theft and abuse of personal identity particulars and the fraudulent manipulation of electronic data to commit theft. At the level of state security, instances of data destruction through electronically transmitted malicious software have been reported. A common thread connecting these activities is the intrusive abuse of computers.

Ironically, improvements in the speed of accessing the Internet have escalated the cyber crime risk.

The primary source of risk is the increase in the number of people sharing information through Internet-facilitated social networking and the phenomenal growth in the use of computer devices in the form of smart mobile phones. Since 2010, the number of users has grown, partly in direct proportion to the increase in the number of social websites such as Facebook and LinkedIn, as well as the BlackBerry messenger service, and partly as a result of greater access to smartphones. Figures released in February 2012 showed that global sales of mobile phones had escalated from 1.391 billion in 2010 to 1.546 billion by the end of 2011. By that stage there were 5.9 billion mobile phone service subscribers. South Africa, which boasts 4 mobile phone service providers, has around 42.3 million subscribers. Current figures show that at least 65% of South African households have access to a cellular telephone on contract, compared to only 20% access to a home-based landline. The highest concentration is in Gauteng, with 48% of adults having access. Other provinces fall within the range of 43% for the Western Cape, and the lowest penetration of 24% in the Eastern Cape, according to forensics expert Craig du Plooy.

The nature of the information transmitted through smartphones appears to be entirely up to the user. There is a high probability that users are not aware of the potential criminal uses of some of the personal information transmitted. Contact addresses and status updates, if intercepted, can be as strategically important to a fraudster as information solicited by and provided to websites of unverified integrity. Information-stealing malicious software (malware) has become quite common, but is not generally known to smartphone users.

At this point, awareness of risks and how to mitigate them does not appear to be spreading as quickly as the escalation in the use of cyber technology.

Risk Factors

Ironically, improvements in the speed of accessing the Internet have escalated the cyber crime risk. With the increase in broadband access, greater opportunities for cyber fraud arise. Faster access encourages more use of the Internet, but also increases the chances for data interception. The SEACOM cable operator has reportedly increased bandwidth internationally by ten times since its transcontinental network came into operation midway through 2009.

Risk also arises from the use of unprotected computer devices. An unprotected computer which is connected to the Internet is a weak link that exposes the entire system to worm-borne attacks. Unprotected computers in the hands of users with inadequate or no training unwittingly raises the risk of cyber attacks on an unlimited range of other connected computers. It is a risk pertaining not just to smartphones, but also to computers donated to charities or to schools.

The use of data storage cards, such as credit and debit cards, is being encouraged in many economies striving to move away from cash-dominated transactions. It is perhaps most common in Africa's tourist hubs. Over the years, cyber criminals have targeted data storage cards as media from which to 'harvest' financial account information. Card cloning is proving to be a resilient form of criminality in South Africa. The statistics on distribution are however scanty. Anecdotes from reported crimes do however show a strong representation of the hospitality sector, especially restaurants in the Western Cape, among the targeted establishments. Analyses by institutions such as the South African Banking Risk Information Centre (SABRIC) highlight the concentric structure of crime networks implicated in card cloning. On the fringes are relatively lowly paid casual workers, mostly serving as waiters or waitresses, recruited by knowledgeable runners who instruct them to collect data from credit and debit cards using portable scanners. The collected data is subsequently transferred to cloned cards for use in commercial transactions or for fund withdrawals. Data captured from compromised auto teller machines is not as common as that which is manually assisted, but it remains an area of exposure.

Reducing Cyber Crime

Knowledge is vital in preempting and minimising cyber crime. In 2010, the South African government declared cyber security to be a national security priority. The declaration reinforced the official resolve underlying the three main applicable statutes, namely the Interception and Monitoring Prohibition Act (1992), the Prevention of Organised Crime Act (1998) and the Electronic Communications and Transactions Act (2002). The legislation is broad enough to penalise unlawful interception and monitoring of e-mail and text messages. While the law might be in place, the reality is that its effectiveness depends on its intended beneficiaries being aware of how to use it and when.

Technological Use in South Africa

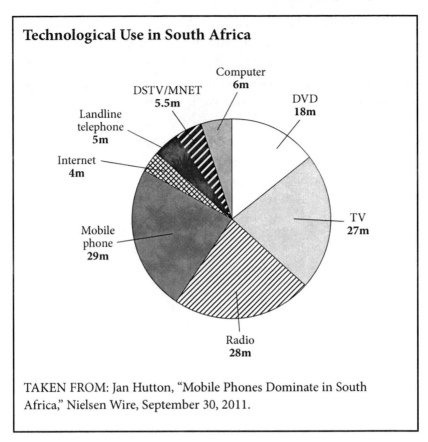

TAKEN FROM: Jan Hutton, "Mobile Phones Dominate in South Africa," Nielsen Wire, September 30, 2011.

At this point, awareness of risks and how to mitigate them does not appear to be spreading as quickly as the escalation in the use of cyber technology. It is largely confined to governments, and the senior levels of larger users of e-technology, such as the financial industry. In 2006 the African Information Security Association (AISA) was established to promote knowledge and create awareness about computer security and cyber crime. The United Nations African Institute for the Prevention of Crime and the Treatment of Offenders (UNAFRI) launched the African Center for Cyberlaw and Cybercrime Prevention (ACCP) in Kampala, Uganda, in August 2010 in response to mobile phone banking. The ACCP set itself the ambitious task of monitoring cyberspace abuses and the incidence of cyber crime in Africa.

More information is required on forms and trends of cyber crime. This might stimulate an improvement in cyber crime reports, which will enable better databases to be compiled. Enhanced databases can support more proactive investigation, as well as the identification of crime networks. Given the rapid proliferation of smartphones, it is suggested that all users should be informed of the main risks and realities. Simultaneously, service providers should be required to appropriately secure all devices they distribute.

In Singapore, Young Adult Males Are Especially Vulnerable to Cybercrime

Ellyne Phneah

Ellyne Phneah is a writer for ZDNet Asia who covers tech issues and tech security. In the following viewpoint, she reports that a recent study showed that Singapore has a high susceptibility to cybercrime. Within Singapore, young men are particularly vulnerable. Phneah says this is because men are more likely to talk to strangers online and are also more likely to view adult content, which may make them vulnerable to viruses or malware. Phneah adds that young people are more vulnerable because they spend more time on the Internet and may be more willing to take risks online. Singapore's population in general has increasing vulnerability, she says, because of rising Internet and mobile cell phone usage.

As you read, consider the following questions:

1. What difference does Phneah report in Internet habits between "millennials" and "boomers"?
2. Which country topped the global list of nations experiencing cybercrime, and what percentage of its people had been victims?

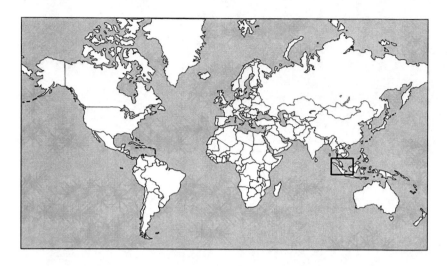

3. What mobile platform is more vulnerable to cyber threat, according to Phneah, and why?

The city-state [of Singapore] is one of the most susceptible in the world to Internet dangers, with the typical cyber-crime victim a male Singaporean born between 1980 and 1993, according to the Norton "Cybercrime Report 2011."

Online Habits and Vulnerability

The new Symantec report, which studied 500 Singaporean adults, found that 86 percent of men are likely to be a victim of cybercrime, compared to women, at 74 percent.

Effendy Ibrahim, consumer business director at Symantec Asia, attributed this finding to specific characteristics. Men were more likely to communicate with strangers online, download malicious software and "look at adult content," he explained during a media briefing on Wednesday [in September 2011].

The study found that 72 percent of Singaporean men downloaded computer viruses or malware [software created to disrupt computers] compared to women at 57 percent. Four times as many Singaporean men, at 23 percent, also viewed adult content online as compared to 6 percent of women.

Additionally, "millennials" [born between 1980 and the present] were more willing than "boomers," or baby boomers [born between 1946 and 1964], to "take a gamble" when it comes to Internet dangers, said Symantec. Globally, "millennials," or Internet users aged between 18 and 31, spent an average of 35 hours online per week, of which 85 percent is devoted to social networking. Eighty-seven percent of their Internet access is via free Wi-Fi connectivity.

---

86 percent of men are likely to be a victim of cybercrime, compared to women, at 74 percent.

"'Millennials' have used technology since a young age and grew up using it," Ibrahim noted, adding that the statistics have led Symantec to conclude that "millennial males" are most at risk when it comes to cybercrime.

Globally, Singapore was one of the top six economies in terms of cybercrime victims, along with emerging markets China, India, South Africa, Mexico and Brazil.

The study involved 20,000 Internet users across 24 countries. Besides China, India and Singapore, Hong Kong and Japan were the other Asian markets surveyed.

As in the case of Brazil and India, eight in 10 users in Singapore indicated they had been victims in their lifetime, compared to last year's finding of 70 percent and the 2011 global average of 74 percent.

China, which topped the global list, has a score of 85 percent, while 84 percent of Internet users in South Africa and 83 percent in Mexico reported to have fallen prey to cyber attacks.

Nearly half, or 45 percent, of Singaporeans surveyed said they need the Internet in their daily lives, making them susceptible to Internet dangers. In particular, 28 percent indicated that they could not live without the web, while 36 percent of social network members said they would lose contact with their friends without social networks.

Despite the hunger for Internet activities, 43 percent of Singaporean adults indicated they do not have an up-to-date security software suite to protect their personal information online. At the same time, less than half, or 49 percent, do not review their credit card statements regularly and 59 percent don't use complex passwords or change them regularly.

"There is a serious disconnect in how people view the threat of cybercrime," Ibrahim added in a statement. "While 94 percent of Singaporeans agree that more needs to be done to bring cybercriminals to justice, fighting cybercrime is a shared responsibility. It requires us all to be more alert and invest in our online smarts and safety."

One in 10 adults globally have experienced mobile-related cybercrime.

Cybercrime cost Singapore US$891 million in 2010, while the damage globally clocked in at US$388 billion.

Computer viruses or malware remain the most common cybercrime category, with a share of 64 percent. Eighteen percent were online threats by sexual predators and 16 percent were online scams.

The Age of Mobile

In its report, Symantec noted the future is "increasingly mobile," with 44 percent of global respondents using their mobile phones to access the Internet. This paves the way for more mobile-related cybercrimes especially in countries with a higher mobile Internet population.

One in 10 adults globally have experienced mobile-related cybercrime, the security vendor found.

Over in Singapore, 69 percent of handset owners accessed the Internet via their mobiles, but only 15 percent have updated security software installed in their devices.

At the sidelines of the briefing, Ibrahim told ZDNet Asia that as long as a mobile device is able to access a website, its user would be "susceptible to threat." Google Android, being an open platform [meant to be modified by third-party software], is more vulnerable to mobile cybercrime, compared with Research in Motion's BlackBerry and Apple's iOS [mobile operating system], he said.

However, even though the mobile threat has increased due to the "explosive growth of mobile devices," attacks on PCs [personal computers] and laptops are still "here to stay," warned Ibrahim.

Women Are Especially Vulnerable to Cybercrime in Pakistan

Zofeen Ebrahim

Zofeen Ebrahim is a Karachi-based journalist who has written for the News International, Dawn, *and Inter Press Service. In the following viewpoint, she reports that women in Pakistan are especially vulnerable to cyber attack because the culture stigmatizes them when they are abused. Pakistani men may target women by creating lewd, photoshopped images of them, or in one extreme instance, by raping a woman and posting video of the incident online. Ebrahim says the problem is exacerbated by the fact that Pakistani women often have limited access to the web and therefore do not know how to protect themselves online. She adds that Pakistan's legal system does not have laws adequately targeting cybercrime.*

As you read, consider the following questions:

1. How does Nighat Dad say that women have become victims of cyber pornography?
2. According to Ebrahim, why are developing countries more vulnerable to cybercrime?

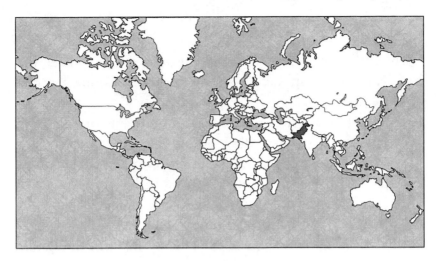

3. Why does Ebrahim say that authorities and activists may have their hands full with cybercrime and harassment issues for years to come?

The Grade 10 student was first drugged, and then four men raped her. The group then apparently tried to extort money from her family. When the family filed a complaint with the police instead, the extortionists in October [2010] then posted a cell phone video of her whole ordeal on the Internet.

Easy Targets

The crime is horrific enough to catch the attention of anyone, as is the act of uploading a video of it on the World Wide Web. But what is also making rights advocates sit up here in Pakistan is the fact that the victim's family had actually come forward to report the crime.

After all, says stalking victim turned activist Fariha Akhtar, "We prefer being abused and harassed than being 'dishonoured' in the eyes of society". That is why, she says, women have become easy targets for cyber crimes in this male-dominated South Asian society.

In the last few years, Pakistan has been catching up with the rest of the world in getting wired, which has not only opened up the country to more business opportunities, but has also livened up social communications among families and friends.

But technology has aided the commitment of crimes as well, with many of these directed towards women. According to special public prosecutor Nighat Dad, women have become victims of cyber pornography and 'morphed' or 'photoshopped' lewd photos of them are uploaded onto the net or passed around through mobile phones.

There are no hard figures to come by for this, though, in part because the victims are too ashamed to lodge a formal complaint.

Akhtar also explains, "Since technology is considered a guy thing, they are given more opportunities to toy with it, leaving women with very limited knowledge to even stay safe while using it, combined with the orders to keep silent should they experience abuse."

Indeed, the Islamabad-based think tank Institute of Policy Studies says there were 412 recorded cases of cyber crime in 2007 to 2009 alone. Yet not one of those is apparently regarding violence against a woman. Says the institute: "(Violence) against women and even their pornographic presentation do not have a mention in the list of cyber crimes in Pakistan."

And yet the cyber crimes may not even be as cruel as what happened to the Grade 10 student for it to affect female victims deeply.

Three years ago, for example, then 27-year-old Zara (not her real name) thought she had it all. A business graduate, she had just been promoted in the telecommunications company where she worked and had a doting fiancé by her side.

But then a male colleague posted photos of Zara purportedly in the nude on the company website. Recalls her sister: "Her life came crumbling down."

The culprit was eventually caught, and he admitted to having photoshopped Zara's photographs to appear she was naked. He said he wanted to teach her a lesson for "not sharing some data" with him.

"Her boss implored her not to resign," says Zara's sister. "But she could not continue in that company knowing her co-workers had seen those pictures. Word spread and her fiancé broke off the engagement."

No Means of Prosecution

Experts in the field say that developing countries like Pakistan are more vulnerable to cyber crimes than other nations. Shahzad Ahmad of Bytes for All (B4A), which works towards Internet governance and rights, says the main reason for this is the "non-existent legal structures".

But then a male colleague posted photos of Zara purportedly in the nude on the company website. Recalls her sister: "Her life came crumbling down."

While there used to be a Prevention of Electronic Crimes Ordinance, this lapsed in November 2009. So, Akhtar says, even if cyber criminals are caught, there is no way of prosecuting them. "At least not for the cyber aspect of their crime," she says.

Ahmad also says the judiciary is incapable of appreciating the "intricacies of such crimes".

Akhtar concedes that authorities have at least started tackling harassment through mobile telephones to some extent. But she says that while counselling a girl whose fake profiles were continuously being created on Facebook, she found out that the state agency she had referred the victim to had its website hacked.

"It left me wondering if they would be of any help," she says of the National Response Centre for Cyber Crimes.

Akhtar says the typical profile of a cyber criminal is usually someone who knows the victim or victims with whom he or she had had some altercation. She adds that in the majority of the cases she has come across, the perpetrator is male.

She remembers only one case where the cyber harassers turned out to be females: "They were a group of young girls from the upmarket schools in Karachi."

She and other rights activists are now closely watching the Grade 10 student's case, which has led to a spate of media reports of similar incidents.

Akhtar, who got involved in the Take Back the Tech campaign launched in 2009, has been "blogging, tweeting, (and) writing articles in local tech magazines on safe and secure use of ICTs (information and communications technology)". She also offers help and guidance to cyber crime victims through the use of the same ICTs.

Authorities and activists like Akhtar may have their hands full for years to come. Mobile phones have already reached the most remote villages in Pakistan, where there are now 100 million mobile phone users, says the Pakistan Telecommunication Authority. There are also 18 million Internet users so far in this country of 175 million people.

Cybercrime Concerns Grow in China

Kathrin Hille

Kathrin Hille is a Financial Times *correspondent based in Beijing. In the following viewpoint, she reports that hacking and computer crimes are a huge and growing problem in China. In part, she says, this is simply because China has a large population, but it is also because China's legal system is poorly equipped to handle hacking. At the moment, Chinese hacking is mostly focused on online gaming: Hackers steal players' virtual goods and then sell them for real money. However, Hille reports, there is fear that hackers may at some point turn their focus to online banking or international espionage.*

As you read, consider the following questions:

1. According to Eagle Wan, how many hackers are there in China, and what kind of skills do they have?
2. How does Hille define a Trojan horse?
3. What is the "black gold value chain," according to Liu Deliang?

The online advertisement from a Beijing student was exactly the kind of message that worries companies in China.

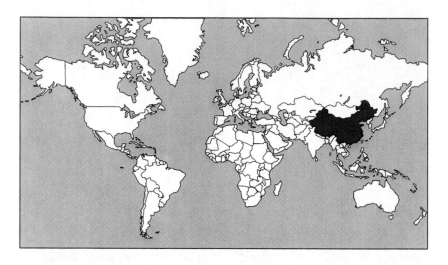

"Taking disciples . . . I do remote control, cracking passwords . . . If needed, contact QQ406842807."

Posted on a Chinese computer hacking forum, the offer was just one of thousands of similar solicitations on the Internet in China. The problem—which Google was reminded of recently—is that people are increasingly taking up the offers.

Cybersecurity specialists say China, with the world's biggest Internet population with about 400m users, probably boasts the planet's largest group of hackers.

China last month became the biggest source of targeted hacking attacks, according to a report by MessageLabs, a research arm of Symantec. The security company says just over a quarter of malicious e-mails sent to gain access to sensitive data came from China.

"There are probably no more than 1,000 people in China who are capable of producing genuinely new tools," says Eagle Wan, a veteran Chinese hacker who now works for IBM. "But those with basic training who can tweak and use tools are in their hundreds of thousands."

Google cited hacking from China as one reason it recently moved its Chinese search engine from the mainland to Hong Kong. Separately, last week hackers broke into the Yahoo e-mail accounts of dozens of China experts. The Foreign Correspondents' Club of China was also forced to close its website after a series of "denial of service" attacks.

While the US and Europe have focused on the intelligence-gathering side of Chinese hacking, the problem has gained more currency inside China, where attacks on foreign nationals are just a fraction of the total online intrusions. Chinese officials and Internet experts insist that the bulk of these are criminal, not political, activities.

According to the China Internet Network Information Center, the state-owned domain name registrar, just over half of China's "netizens" encountered Internet security incidents last year. Most cases involved viruses and Trojan horses—disguised malicious software that facilitates unauthorised access to the recipient's computer—while surfing the web. It said one-fifth of users suffered financially.

China ... probably boasts the planet's largest group of hackers.

Mr Wan, who remains close to the Chinese hacking community, says the landscape has undergone a radical change since his early days. He remains closely involved in the Chinese hacking community through Netersky, an online community he founded to translate hackers' knowledge into Internet security enhancement.

"In the 1990s, when the Internet in China was just starting up, we were patriotic hackers," he recalls. "But now, most people are in it for the money."

Some veteran hackers are now designing, tweaking and selling Trojans since it is the only thing they know, says Mr Wan. They have helped create a new industry of criminal hackers who—just like the suppliers, integrators, traders and service providers that make up China's manufacturing sector—have become highly specialised.

China and the Internet Police

The Internet poses a 'dual use problem' for the Chinese government. On the one hand, the Internet is recognised as an essential tool in today's information economy. On the other hand, the Chinese government worries that losing control of the tool may not only harm the security and order of the Internet but may also have spillover effects on the real world, perhaps even jeopardizing the legitimacy of the [Communist] Party or government to rule. To manage the potentially negative effects of the Internet and harness the Internet to strengthen its rule, the Chinese government has made great efforts to regulate the Internet.

Among the regulatory efforts of the Chinese government has been the formation of an Internet police force.... The Chinese government regards the Internet as an electronic public space in which a police force is needed to keep order. Law and order are important to the Chinese psyche. While Internet censorship, particularly of political expression, does exist, the Chinese government is also attempting to harness the Internet to bring popular grievances into official channels. The Internet police and the regulatory mechanisms are therefore intended to frame online content so that it is consistent with leadership goals and thereby ensure that the Internet will not become a public space separate from the [Communist] Party state.

Xiaoyan Chen and Peng Hwa Ang,
"The Internet Police in China: Regulation, Scope and Myths,"
Online Society in China: Creating, Celebrating
and Instrumentalising the Online Carnival.
Eds. David Kurt Herold and Peter Marolt. New York:
Routledge, 2011, p. 40.

"We call it the 'black gold value chain,'" says Liu Deliang, director of the Asia-Pacific Institute for Cyber-Law Studies in Beijing.

Mr Liu says China's love affair with online gaming and virtual worlds over the past eight years has helped the growth of the virtual value chain.

China's legal system is unfit to battle cybercrime.

"Large numbers of people have amassed virtual goods, and whenever there's an accumulation of wealth, there will be people trying to steal it," he says.

Mr Liu says one problem is that China's legal system is unfit to battle cybercrime. Aside from the fact that Chinese police are organised along regional lines, which makes little sense in the cyber world, China does not have enough cyber-savvy cops chasing the growing number of online thieves and hackers.

He also warns that cybercrime has still not reached its potential as a business because hackers are still focused on stealing virtual goods and currency.

"[Chinese hackers] haven't even moved on to targeting online banking on a major scale, let alone the international market. There's just too rich a harvest for them here right now."

James Lewis, a cybersecurity expert at the Center for Strategic and International Studies in Washington, who leads a fledgling dialogue on cybersecurity with Chinese academics and government representatives, says the Chinese government sees hacking mainly as a cybercrime issue.

Chinese authorities insist that domestic hackers are engaged in crime, not international spying. However, given the number of people involved in the various links of the "black gold value chain", there is plenty of opportunity for Chinese intelligence to engage in espionage.

Mr Wan rejects that as highly unlikely and says he has never been in contact with government officials. "But yes, you cannot exclude that possibility," he says.

Canadian Banks Look to Insurance to Decrease Vulnerability to Cybercrime

John Greenwood

John Greenwood is a financial services reporter at the Financial Post. *In the following viewpoint, he reports that most financial institutions in Canada are reluctant to disclose or report incidents of hacking. He says that institutions fear that disclosure will encourage other hackers, and it may also scare away customers. Greenwood says banks have hesitated to take out insurance against hacking because the insurance would require them to disclose more information than they are prepared to do. However, Greenwood concludes, as government regulations around disclosure become more strict, and as incidents of hacking increase, banks are likely to move more and more toward greater disclosure and more insurance.*

As you read, consider the following questions:

1. What high-profile cybercrime incidents does Greenwood list as changing the Canadian market in cybercrime insurance?

2. According to Greenwood, how has cybercrime changed since laws were first developed to deal with it?

John Greenwood, "Canadian Banks Beefing Up Insurance Against Hacker Attacks," *Financial Post*, July 28, 2012. www.financialpost.com. Material reprinted with the express permission of: National Post, a division of Postmedia Network Inc.

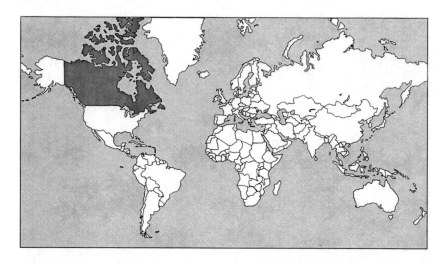

3. What does Greenwood say is one of the biggest challenges for institutions victimized by cybercrime?

Canadian banks have long been reluctant to talk about losses from cyber attacks.

Disclosure and Insurance

Rick Waugh, chief executive of the Bank of Nova Scotia, said in an interview earlier this year [in 2012] that's partly because disclosing details of a successful network break-in would be like giving a road map to the bad guys.

Another plausible explanation for the banks' reticence might have to do with reputation: By owning up, a bank is admitting it could be vulnerable and potentially providing customers with a reason to leave.

But whether or not they want to talk about it, banks are increasingly buying insurance to protect against losses from computer breaches.

"Everybody's worried about it, especially financial institutions, because a lot of the information they have is very sensitive," said Michael Petersen, a practice leader at Marsh Canada.

Mr. Petersen said the Canadian market is "rapidly evolving" and has been for the past five years, especially in the wake of a string of high-profile incidents ranging from rogue employees at tax haven banks selling customer account information, to garden variety debit card theft, to a full-scale network break-in at New York–based Citigroup affecting hundreds of thousands of account holders across North America.

Disclosing details of a successful network break-in would be like giving a road map to the bad guys.

There are now more than 26 underwriters offering such policies designed specifically for the financial sector, including Chubb Corp., ACE Ltd., Chartis and Kiln Group Ltd., compared with barely a handful 10 years ago.

"Every organization is trying to figure out their exposure and the potential losses they could face," Mr. Petersen said. "When you assess your risk you have to both look outside the organization and within. You have to take a close look at your employees to ensure incidents don't occur, but even with all that mistakes happen, memory sticks can be stolen. . . ."

Annual cyber risk insurance premiums for the United States alone are worth as much as $1 billion a year, according to analyst estimates.

Changing Risks, Changing Regulations

The federal Privacy Commissioner [of Canada] has guidelines requiring organizations to notify affected customers following a breach in which personal information is stolen, but there's no rule about broader public disclosure. Presumably, securities rules around disclosure of material events would cover major network break-ins but such events are rarely, if ever, mentioned in financial reports or press releases by financial companies. That may be about to change.

Last fall, the U.S. Securities and Exchange Commission announced that public companies of all kinds must disclose de-

---

Cybercrime and Disclosure

No one really knows the extent of cybercrime as many crimes go unreported. Most companies that have been the victim of cybercrime simply won't talk to the press, although . . . many states have passed data disclosure laws that require disclosure to those affected. The concern of companies who are victims of cybercrime is loss of public trust and image—not to mention the fear of encouraging copycat hackers. In 2007, the FBI [Federal Bureau of Investigation] received 206,844 complaints of cybercrime committed over the Internet, with losses estimated at $240 million. The actual cost of cybercrime is certainly much higher because not all crimes are reported and not all the costs (legal fees, loss of revenue, etc.) to companies affected by data breaches can be accurately estimated. The cost of the TJX data breach for example [in which the apparel chain had customer data stolen in 2006], is estimated to have cost the firm over $256 million in loss of business and legal fees.

George W. Reynolds,
Information Technology for Managers.
Boston, MA: Cengage Learning, 2010, p. 343.

---

tails of all network breaches resulting in material losses, including the actual costs to the company as well as the nature of the attack.

Meanwhile, at least 46 states have brought in similar legislation of their own.

"There has been an evolution of the laws in the U.S. but here in Canada disclosure requirements aren't as broad," said Mr. Petersen, who added that "over time" he anticipates that lawmakers in this country will follow suit with the tougher rules being put in place south of the border.

But even in the U.S., the rules around what companies need to do after a cyber attack are a work in progress—largely because the technology itself is changing and developing so quickly. Back when many of today's laws were first mapped out, computer hacking was mostly a nuisance activity carried out by bored teenagers looking to deface a website or, at worst, disable an e-commerce portal.

"Ninety-nine percent of the time it's the customer that gets hit."

Today, many of the hackers are sophisticated criminals bent on stealing money or financial information; financial companies are spending a lot more to defend themselves.

Often, one of the biggest challenges for victims is to determine the extent of the damage—what information has been taken, how many customers are affected and so on. Sometimes, it takes days or even weeks before there are clear answers to those questions.

Typically, in the case of banks, it's the customers that are targeted first and the hackers then use the stolen passwords to break into their accounts, according to José Fernandez, a software engineering professor at École Polytechnique de Montréal.

"Ninety-nine percent of the time it's the customer that gets hit," he said, adding that credible loss estimates for North America are probably in the low billions of dollars.

So far, he suspects, most banks are willing to cover the cost themselves without relying on insurance.

That's because taking out insurance and making claims would involve a higher level of disclosure than players are comfortable with.

But with the increase in hacking incidents and higher losses that may soon change.

Periodical and Internet Sources Bibliography

The following articles have been selected to supplement the diverse views presented in this chapter.

Shahid Abbasi	"Pakistan Facing Legal Vacuum Since Lapse of Cybercrimes Ordinance in 2009," The News Tribe, August 31, 2012. www.thenewstribe.com.
BBC News	"China Arrests Thousands in Latest Internet Crime Crackdown," July 26, 2012.
Emily Chung	"Canada a Favourite for Cybercrime," CBC News, May 11, 2011.
Steve Gold	"Cybercriminals Exploit Japan Earthquake Anguish," *E&T*, March 17, 2011.
Graeme McMillan	"Japan Criminalized Cybercrime: Make a Virus, Get Three Years in Jail," *Time*, June 17, 2011.
NielsenWire	"Mobile Phone Penetration in Indonesia Triples in Five Years," February 23, 2011. http://blog.nielsen.com.
Rachel Olding	"Clueless Vulnerable to Cyber Crime," *Canberra Times* (Australia), September 7, 2012.
Ellyne Phneah	"Average Singaporean Loses More Money to Cybercrime," ZDNet.com, September 6, 2012.
Dewi Safitri	"Why Is Indonesia So in Love with the Blackberry?," BBC News, June 15, 2011.
Allen Smith	"'Wild West' of Cyber Insurance Might Cover Spear Phishing, Other Cybercrime," Society for Human Resource Management, February 8, 2012.

GLOBALVIEWPOINTS

CHAPTER 2

Law and Cybercrime

Thailand's Cybercrime Law Stifles Freedom of Speech

Lynette Lee Corporal

Lynette Lee Corporal is a Thailand-based journalist for Inter Press Service. In the following viewpoint, she reports that Thailand has passed a cybercrime law and has been using the law to crack down on political speech in the name of security. Corporal says that websites critical of the government have been shut down, and people who have criticized the government online have been prosecuted. She also worries that the crackdown will have a chilling effect on free speech, causing many Thais to censor themselves for fear of government reprisals. She concludes that the government does not understand the new Internet culture, in which sharing and free speech are crucial.

As you read, consider the following questions:

1. According to Chiranuch Premchaiporn, what is the main problem with the cybercrime law?

2. Why is it hard to tell how many people have been charged under Thailand's cybercrime law, according to independent media lawyer Sinfah Tunsarawuth?

3. Why does Corporal say that Prachatai is closing down its controversial web board?

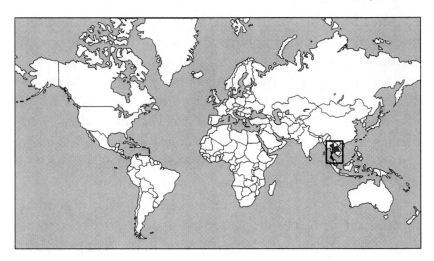

Many netizens [active participants on the Internet] worldwide have long realised that the Internet is not completely without fetters, but those in Thailand say a three-year-old law is now practically choking Thai self-expression and right to information in cyberspace.

Websites Blocked, Discussion Stifled

More to the point, Thai netizens, journalists and media advocates say that the country's authorities have taken advantage of ambiguities in the [Computer] Crime Act (CCA) to censor or close down altogether websites or forums that the government deems "offensive".

Critics say that the government has been on an intensive cyber crackdown in the last two years.

"The problem with the cyber crime law is its lack of clarity, which leaves it wide open to misinterpretation," Chiranuch Premchaiporn, director of the yet-to-be-unblocked independent news website Prachatai ('Free People'), told a discussion here this week [July 2010] to review and propose amendments to the law.

Already, reports of prosecution under the computer crime law have driven much political discussion underground. Others worry this is discouraging people from debating key issues in the public sphere, especially amid the political divisions in Thailand that led to the largest protests in decades by the anti-government United Front for Democracy Against Dictatorship and the military's subsequent crackdown in May.

Already, "the authorities' actions are driving the growth of underground forums and space," adds Chiranuch.

The actions of Thailand's online censors "will cause people to drop off from the discussion of issues", agrees Southeast Asian Press Alliance executive director Roby Alampay. "Only the truly determined and technologically savvy will continue to find ways to express their voices online," he adds.

Critics say that the government has been on an intensive cyber crackdown in the last two years [that is, 2008–2010]. The international media watchdog Reporters Without Borders says that in July 2009 alone, the Information and Communications Technology (ICT) Ministry, citing threats to national security, blocked more than 16,944 websites.

Internet freedom activists say that as of this year, the number has reached more than 50,000, adding that it is difficult to get a clear figure of exactly how many websites have been blocked.

Likewise, "it is difficult to say how many have been charged under the CCA," said independent media lawyer Sinfah Tunsarawuth. "There are at least 10, but we don't know if there are more as defendants don't want to talk and would rather settle out of court. It's also difficult to track down individual court cases."

Thailand, a country of 68 million people, has 13.4 million Internet users, with 113 Internet service providers (ISPs) licensed as of July 2009.

Netizens say the CCA has enabled authorities to step up the online clampdown. Other regulations in place that affect the online community and media include the emergency decree that the government imposed in April and remains in effect in Bangkok and several provinces, and which allows it to shut websites deemed too detrimental to security.

Among the websites that have been blocked since April is Prachatai. Even before that, Chiranuch herself was charged with violating Section 15 of the Computer Crime Act for postings made on Prachatai's web board that were allegedly in breach of the lese majeste law [that is, a law that protects the dignity of the state].

"They think that control or shutting down websites, for instance, gives more security but, in fact, reflects insecurity."

CCA critics also cite the law's Section 14 as being problematic. It covers offences such as the uploading of material deemed "likely to" threaten any person as well as national security or sow panic among the public, Sinfah's report says.

Security and Insecurity

"If anyone is seen as 'likely to' harm national security, it doesn't have to happen but that person is already liable," he told IPS [Inter Press Service] recently. Against the backdrop of legal restrictions on expression, Thai Netizen Network [TNN] committee member Sarinee Achavanuntakul says that there is a need to distinguish between threats to national security and the expression of opinion. "We should be able to define what constitutes dangerous content," she says.

But one hindrance to this, says Thai Journalists Association president Prasong Lertratanawisute, is that implementing bodies such as the ICT can easily be "led by political agendas".

Political analyst Suranand Vejjajiva adds that the Thai authorities' notion of control is through the use of propaganda. "The bureaucratic system has so many laws, rules and

Prime Minister Thaksin and the Internet

While Internet filtering has been actively practiced in Thailand since 2002, it did not become a political issue until after the military coup d'état of September 19, 2006. The coup overthrew the highly popular Prime Minister Thaksin Shinawatra and marked the beginning of a tumultuous chapter in Thai political history. In the aftermath of the coup, the self-exiled Thaksin and his red-shirt supporters have exploited the Internet as a primary channel for political communication. Meanwhile, much political expression in Thailand has resorted to cyberspace, which has enjoyed relatively greater freedom of expression than have other forms of mass media. While broadcast media in Thailand have historically been controlled through state monopoly of the airwaves, and print media generally had a lukewarm attitude toward the coup, throughout the post-coup period (which international observers call color-coded politics for its red and yellow shirts), the Internet has emerged as a major public sphere. Different online political forums, online newspapers, and political websites have become important platforms for expression, exchanges, and debates that represent a wide spectrum of political ideologies and orientations. As a result, authorities have increasingly zeroed in on Internet content as a target for censorship and surveillance in the post-2006-coup period.

Pirongrong Ramasoota, "Internet Politics in Thailand After the 2006 Coup," Access Contested: Security, Identity, and Resistance in Asian Cyberspace. *Eds. Ronald Deibert, John Palfrey, Rafal Rohozinski, and Jonathan Zittrain. Cambridge, MA: MIT Press, 2012, p. 85.*

regulations that give universal power to the person holding office," he also says. "They think that control or shutting down websites, for instance, gives more security but, in fact, reflects insecurity."

TNN's Sarinee believes as well that the government does not really understand the nature of the Internet and that, unlike the more traditional forms of media, it simply is impossible to censor it.

At the same time, she worries that "unless you make it a very personal thing" and show people how censorship affects their own lives, they would not care to react to the government's current sweep through the web.

Prachatai, however, seems to be waving a white flag, and is closing down its controversial web board at the end of July. Chiranuch, who says past comments on the board have led to the arrest of several people, explains, "We don't want to mislead users that we can protect them online."

"We'd rather shut down the web board than collect our users' personal data," she also says, referring to a provision in the law that directs Internet providers to collect and store online users' personal information for 90 days.

Comments Suranand: "Sharing is the heart of the new Internet culture where everybody is a stakeholder. Unfortunately, the government and other organisations can't seem to come to grips with this and are refusing to understand that the world has changed."

France's Cybercrime Laws May Threaten Internet Freedom

Stefan Simons

Stefan Simons is the Paris correspondent for Spiegel. *In the following viewpoint, he reports that France is preparing to pass a package of laws called LOPPSI 2. The laws are intended to crack down on Internet crime and particularly on online pedophilia. Simons argues that the laws are intended to show that French president Nicolas Sarkozy is tough on crime, helping him regain popularity. However, Simons says, civil rights and opposition groups have claimed that the law infringes on freedom of speech and should not be passed.*

As you read, consider the following questions:

1. What responsibilities does LOPPSI 2 give to Internet service providers?
2. Besides Internet regulations, what else does Simons say is part of the bundle of legislation in LOPPSI 2?
3. Who is Sandrine Bélier, and what is her objection to LOPPSI 2, according to Simons?

The lower house of the French parliament has approved a draft bill that will allow the state unprecedented control over the Internet. Although the government says it will im-

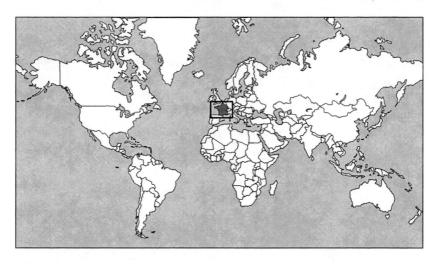

prove security for ordinary citizens, civil rights activists are warning of a "new level" of censorship and surveillance.

LOPPSI 2

For members of the French administration, it is a law against digital crime. For civil rights activists and politicians from opposition parties, it is a plan for censorship that excites fear and loathing—and even conjures up the specter of Big Brother [the symbol of state power in George Orwell's dystopian novel *1984*] and the surveillance state.

The lower house of the French parliament, the National Assembly, passed the first draft of the bill, known as "LOPPSI 2," on Tuesday [in February 2010]. It will now go on for a second reading in the Senate, where it seems likely to pass, thanks to the government's majority. If the Senate approves the bill, the new law could come into force as early as this summer. The legislation could have far-reaching consequences: LOPPSI 2 contains rules that would make France the European country where the Internet is subject to the most censorship, regulation, control and surveillance.

The new legislation could in the future force Internet service providers (ISPs) to shut off access to criminal sites, should they be officially instructed to do so. According to the draft legislation, the law "makes it the responsibility of each Internet service provider to ensure that users don't have access to unsuitable content."

Sarkozy is pulling out a presidential trump card. He is hoping that fear of criminals will convince voters to come to the polling booths.

The list of banned websites would be provided by the Interior Ministry. The approach is very similar to a proposed German Internet law aimed at fighting child pornography, which also foresaw limiting access to certain sites. That legislation was signed into law by German president Horst Köhler on Wednesday—even though the German government had recently decided it no longer wanted to apply the law in its existing form, after massive protests by Internet users.

Under the new French legislation, police and security forces would be able to use clandestinely installed software, known in the jargon as a "Trojan horse," to spy on private computers. Remote access to private computers would be made possible under the supervision of a judge.

The draft law indicates that President Nicolas Sarkozy is sticking to his hard line on Internet issues. Last year his administration pushed through the HADOPI law which gives ISPs the power to block or restrict Internet access to users of illegal file-sharing sites who refuse to desist under a "three strikes" system. The new legislation is simply the next step in regulating Internet use in France.

Political Motivations

The French government's hard line should not surprise anyone. In a few weeks' time, regional elections will take place in France. In the 2004 regional elections, Sarkozy's UMP [Union

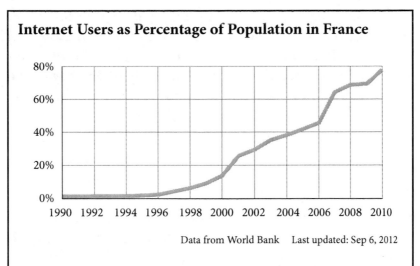

Internet Users as Percentage of Population in France

Data from World Bank   Last updated: Sep 6, 2012

TAKEN FROM: "Internet Users as Percentage of Population, France,"
World Development Indicators and Global Development Finance,
Google Public Data Explorer, September 6, 2012.

for a Popular Movement] party did particularly badly. By
showing himself to be a tough leader, Sarkozy hopes to avoid
history repeating itself and shore up support for his policies.
Polls indicate there is disappointment with his leadership and
his government has low approval ratings. That is the reason
why, in the face of a rampant economic crisis, growing unem-
ployment, a devastatingly large budget deficit and various political scandals, Sarkozy is pulling out a presidential trump
card. He is hoping that fear of criminals will convince voters
to come to the polling booths.

In that respect, there is no more suitable issue than child
pornography on the Internet and the hunt for pedophile
criminals whose only desire is to seduce innocents via their
home computers. According to that argument, it is necessary
to impose controls on the digital world and introduce state
surveillance, so that a proactive Big Brother can fight the cyber world's sexual deviants who are, in all likelihood, lurking
on Facebook or Twitter.

In fact, Internet controls are only part of the bundle of legislation that is included in LOPPSI 2. The various articles include a colorful batch of security measures developed by Interior Minister Brice Hortefeux, a close ally of Sarkozy's, who pushed through the first version of the security laws in 2002.

The new package has been in the works since October 2007 and has, according to Hortefeux, been beefed up by 13 provisions "like in bodybuilding." It is a hodgepodge of different measures, governing issues as disparate as courtroom procedures, traffic laws, defense, sport, integration and even questions regarding burial ordnances in the French territory of New Caledonia in the South Pacific. The French daily *Le Monde* wrote of a "chest with many drawers."

In addition to law enforcement tools for municipal police and private security companies, there is also a provision calling for a tripling of surveillance cameras in France—from 20,000 to 60,000—by 2011. The provision has been described harmlessly as "video protection."

The package also contains harsher penalties for break-ins, assault and drunk driving. Curfews for minors are also to be allowed.

"When it comes to restrictions, this text is preparing us for hell."

"Serious Threat" to Internet Neutrality

Civil rights activists are outraged, as is the opposition. "We are seeing a whole series of lapses and rights limitations," says Jean-Pierre Dubois, president of the French League of Human Rights. Sandrine Bélier, a member of the European Parliament for the Green Party, says the bill represents "a serious threat" to the neutrality of the Internet.

"The filtering and blocking of the web has become a standard weapon in the legislative arsenal of a government which has been shameless in its handling of personal freedoms," Bélier said in an interview with the online edition of the magazine *Marianne*. She complained that policing responsibility was being handed to web providers, despite the lack of a legal basis for doing so. Indeed, it is precisely for this reason that the similar draft law in Germany will likely never come into force.

"LOPPSI has brought us to a new level," Bélier says, adding that "when it comes to restrictions, this text is preparing us for hell."

LOPPSI 2 contains a number of other gifts to French security authorities as well, including improved integration between police files and personal data kept by, for example, banks. The goal, Hortefeux explains innocently, is that of "improving the daily security of French citizens." He says the laws will help to "maintain the level and quality of service provided by domestic security forces."

Iraq's Cybercrime Law Stifles Freedom of Speech

Human Rights Watch

Human Rights Watch (HRW) is an international human rights organization. In the following viewpoint, HRW reports that the Iraqi government is in the process of passing a new law that would regulate Internet crimes. HRW says that the law is worded vaguely and would effectively enable the government to prosecute anyone who criticizes either government or religious leaders over the Internet. HRW concludes that the law is part of the Iraqi government's ongoing effort to restrict freedom of speech and expression. It says that the government should not pass the law.

As you read, consider the following questions:

1. According to HRW, what does article 3 of the new Iraqi crimes law do?
2. What does HRW recommend specifically that the government of Iraq should do about the new law?
3. What behavior of the government of Iraq leads HRW to conclude that the new law would be used to violate freedom of expression?

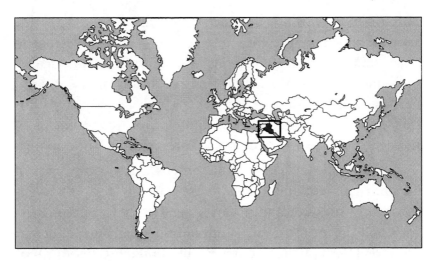

Iraq's government is in the process of enacting what it refers to as an information crimes law to regulate the use of information networks, computers, and other electronic devices and systems. The proposed law had its first reading before Iraq's Council of Representatives on July 27, 2011; a second reading is expected as early as July 2012. As currently drafted, the proposed legislation violates international standards protecting due process, freedom of speech, and freedom of association.

A Vague and Repressive Law

The proposed law states, in article 2, that it aims "to provide legal protection for the legitimate use of computers and information networks, and punish those who commit acts that constitute encroachment on the rights of their users." In particular, the law provides penalties for the use of computers in connection with various prohibited activities, such as financial fraud and misappropriation (article 7), money laundering (article 10), network disruptions (article 14), illicit monitoring (articles 15(1)(b) and 16), and intellectual property violations (article 21). However, the law is not narrowly targeted; rather, its vague provisions would criminalize the use of computers in connection with a wide range of broadly defined activities, many of which are presently unregulated, without reference to any specific criteria. In allowing Iraqi authorities to penalize individuals in this manner, several provisions of the law appear to conflict with international law and the Iraqi Constitution, and if enacted would constitute serious curtailments of the right of Iraqis to freedom of expression and association.

For example, article 3 of the proposed law sets a term of life imprisonment and a large fine against any person who intentionally uses computer devices and an information network for the purpose of: "undermining the independence, unity, or safety of the country, or its supreme economic, political, military, or security interests," or "participating, negotiating, promoting, contracting with, or dealing with a hostile entity in any way with the purpose of disrupting security and public order or endangering the country." Article 6 could provide for life imprisonment and a large fine against any person who uses computer devices and an information network for the purpose of "inflaming sectarian tensions or strife; disturbing security and the public order; or defaming the country;" or "publishing or broadcasting false or misleading events for the purpose of weakening confidence in the electronic financial system, electronic commercial or financial documents, or similar things, or damaging the national economy and financial confidence in the state." Article 21 sets a minimum one-year prison term for "any person who encroaches on any religious, moral, family, or social values or principles or the sanctity of private life using an information network or computer devices in any shape or form." Article 22 provides for a prison sentence and fine "against any person who . . . creates, administers, or helps to create a site on an information network that promotes or incites to licentiousness and obscenity or any programs, information, photographs, or films that infringe on probity or public morals or advocate or propagate such things."

Given the vagueness and breadth of these provisions, as well as the severity of the punishment for the violations, authorities could use the law to punish any expression that they claim constitutes a threat to some governmental, religious, or social interest, or to deter legitimate criticisms of or peaceful challenges to governmental or religious officials or policies.

The draft information crimes law appears to be part of a broad effort to suppress peaceful dissent by criminalizing legitimate activities involving information sharing and networking.

Criminalizing Dissent

Moreover, the government is introducing the law as the use of Internet and social media by journalists and civic and human rights activists has become increasingly important in Iraq, especially in the wake of the uprisings across the Arab world. Given the key role of information technology, devices, and networks in journalism and the dissemination of information and opinions, the proposed law poses a severe threat to independent media, whistleblowers, and peaceful activists.

The proposed information crimes law is part of a broader pattern of restrictions on fundamental freedoms in Iraq, particularly freedom of expression, association, and assembly. In May 2011, the Council of Ministers approved a draft of the Law of Freedom of Expression of Opinion, Assembly, and Peaceful [Protest], which contains provisions that would criminalize peaceful speech, with penalties of up to 10 years in prison.

Since February 2011, Human Rights Watch has documented often violent attacks by Iraqi security forces and gangs, apparently acting with the support of the Iraqi government, against peaceful demonstrators demanding human rights, better services, and an end to corruption. During nationwide demonstrations on February 25, 2011, for example, security forces killed at least 12 protesters across the country and injured more than 100. Iraqi security forces beat unarmed journalists and protesters that day, smashing cameras and confiscating memory cards. On June 10 in Baghdad, government-backed gangs armed with wooden planks, knives, iron pipes, and other weapons beat and stabbed peaceful protesters and sexually molested female demonstrators as security forces stood by and watched, sometimes laughing at the victims.

Given this backdrop, the draft information crimes law appears to be part of a broad effort to suppress peaceful dissent by criminalizing legitimate activities involving information sharing and networking. Iraq's Council of Representatives should insist that the government significantly revise the proposed information crimes law to conform to the requirements of international law, and the council should reject its passage into law in its present form. Without substantial revision, the proposed legislation would sharply undercut both freedom of expression and association.

Recommendations to Iraq's Council of Representatives

- Do not pass the information crimes law until the government of Iraq modifies the proposed legislation to:
    1. Conform to international standards by identifying any prohibited conduct with sufficient specificity, particularly in articles 3, 6, 21, and 22, such that Iraqi citizens will know in advance what conduct is prohibited and subject to punishment;
    2. Comply with international human rights law protecting freedom of expression by (1) clearly identifying any prohibited types of expression, (2) clearly identifying the legitimate threat presented by such expressions, and (3) requiring, in any

individual case, that any punishment (up to the maximum provided) be proportional to the harm caused by the expression; and

3. Comply with international human rights law protecting freedom of association by (1) clearly identifying any prohibited organizations, entities, or activities, and (2) clearly identifying the legitimate threat presented by such organizations, entities, or activities, and (3) ensuring any legal restriction on freedom of association is proportional, in terms of scope, time limitation, and criminal punishment to the harm caused.

Recommendations to the Government of Iraq

- Suspend and then amend penal and civil code provisions and other legislation and regulations to remove or precisely define, in line with international standards of freedom of expression and association, any vaguely expressed restrictions, and to remove excessive penalties on journalists, activists and others, including imprisonment and excessive fines, especially for minor infractions;

- Ensure a speedy, transparent, and fair investigation and prosecution of assaults by security forces and others against journalists and activists, and direct all security forces to end the use of force to intimidate, harass, arrest, assault, or otherwise prevent Iraqis from demonstrating peacefully and journalists from doing their work; and

- Direct government agencies to stop filing politically motivated lawsuits against journalists and their publications.

Violations of Fundamental Due Process Standards

Several provisions of the proposed information crimes law, including some providing for the harshest prison sentences, violate international standards on due process because they fail to provide meaningful notice or guidance to Iraqi citizens, and to journalists and members of organizations operating in Iraq, as to what constitutes criminal behavior.

Among other things, the law threatens life imprisonment and large fines for those found guilty of "inflaming sectarian tensions or strife"; "defaming the country"; "[u]ndermining the independence, unity, or safety of the country, or its supreme economic, political, military, or security interests"; or "[p]ublishing or broadcasting false or misleading events for the purpose of weakening confidence in the electronic financial system, electronic commercial or financial documents, or similar things, or damaging the national economy and financial confidence in the state." The law also imposes imprisonment and a fine on anyone who "encroaches on any religious, moral, family, or social values or principles," or "[c]reates, administers, or helps to create . . . any programs, information, photographs, or films that infringe on probity or public morals or advocate or propagate such things."

These provisions do not prohibit any specific conduct; instead, they rely on vague characterizations whose applications government officials will decide in hindsight without reference to any particular criteria that would guide conduct in advance of any prosecution under the law. Particularly in light of the current political instability in Iraq, it is, to a large extent, impossible to know what might qualify as a transgression. Practically speaking, these provisions would mean that a person could be threatened with life imprisonment for conduct that he or she had no ability to discern in advance would be considered criminal. As a result, the current draft of the law threatens Iraqis and others, including journalists, with arbitrary arrest and detention, and, as discussed below, would deter Iraqis from fully engaging in legitimate, peaceful activities that they fear could subject them to punishment according to this law. If it does not revise these provisions and articulate specific activities that are prohibited, Iraq's Council of Representatives would empower officials to act arbitrarily, and to exercise their authority in a discriminatory fashion against particular individuals or groups.

The proposed information crimes law appears to violate articles 9 and 14 of the International Covenant on Civil and Political Rights (ICCPR) and article 14 of the revised Arab Charter on Human Rights concerning due process, both of which protect rights to liberty and due process.

Indeed, anyone who criticizes or challenges a governmental or religious official . . . could be prosecuted under the law.

Under these provisions of international law, Iraq must provide individuals with procedural and substantive guarantees against arbitrary arrest, detention, conviction, or punishment. The United Nations Human Rights Committee, the body of independent experts charged with interpreting the ICCPR and assessing state compliance with it, has explained that for a law not to be arbitrary it "must be formulated with sufficient precision to enable an individual to regulate his or her conduct accordingly." Accordingly, overly vague laws which fail to guide either individual or official conduct are antithetical to due process and violate the provisions of international law cited above. Citizens must know in advance what specific kinds of conduct could subject them to punishment, and based on what criteria.

Violations of the Right to Freedom of Expression

While both international law and the Iraqi Constitution recognize that limited and clearly specified restrictions on freedom of expression may be justified, certain provisions of the proposed information crimes law do not satisfy any of the criteria that restrictions on freedom of expression must meet to comply with international and Iraqi law: adequate specification by law (that is, the restriction must be "provided by law"); for a legitimate aim (as set out in the ICCPR); proportionality and necessity; and preservation of the "essence" of the freedom. For example, the proposed information crimes law prohibits, and harshly punishes, the communication of expressions that "[u]ndermin[e] the independence, unity, or safety of the country, or its supreme economic, political, military, or security interests;" or that encroach "on any religious, moral, family, or social values or principles."

In order for a restriction to be "provided by law," as that concept is understood within international law, it must satisfy the general due process standards discussed above. That is, it "must be formulated with sufficient precision to enable an individual to regulate his or her conduct accordingly" and it "may not confer unfettered discretion for the restriction of freedom of expression on those charged with its execution." As discussed, various provisions of the proposed information crimes law depend on such overly vague and contentious classifications that they do not meet this threshold standard. Indeed, it appears obvious that the intent behind such provisions is not to define an offense in advance but to give government officials unfettered discretion to make retrospective judgments as to whether they can punish an electronic communication or activity. Accordingly, attempts to enforce such provisions of the draft law would not satisfy the "provided by law" requirement within the meaning of article 19(3) of the ICCPR and would not be "by a law or on the basis of a law" as required by article 46 of the Iraqi Constitution.

Given the vagueness and breadth of the above noted provisions, as well as the severity of the punishment for any violation of such provisions, it is clear that the law is not proportional or designed to address a specific threat. Rather, officials could use the law to suppress any expression that they claim, based on their personal judgment and potentially improper motivation, constitutes a "threat" to some governmental, religious, or social interest. As such, they could determine that innumerable categories of expression, including political expression, could (after the fact) fall within the law's prohibitions. Indeed, anyone who criticizes or challenges a governmental or religious official, department, agency, or policy, or who supports a minority party, organization, or news or opinion medium that criticizes or challenges some aspect of the government or of some protected nongovernmental institution or practice, could be prosecuted under the law.

Given that the provisions of the draft law could be applied to almost any manner of expression that is electronically communicated, rather than just to specifically defined criminal conduct to protect a specific and important public interest, such provisions cannot be characterized as necessary. Moreover, embedded in the law is a disturbing, and illegal, premise that the expression of a politically or morally unpopular idea—no matter how disconnected that expression may be from a specific criminal or terrorist act—is itself something criminal. That premise contravenes well-established principles as to what restrictions on expression may be necessary pursuant to international law; indeed, it is never necessary or permissible to prohibit media outlets, publishers, journalists, websites, or other means of information dissemination from publishing material "solely on the basis that it may be critical of the government or the political social system espoused by the government," or to penalize them for doing so.

The proposed law is problematic also because international norms that allow limited restrictions on freedom of expression do not permit such restrictions for the protection of abstract entities such as religions, beliefs, ideas, or symbols. International law specifically prohibits restrictions on speech based on its damaging or defamatory effects to religions or beliefs. The right to freedom of expression includes the right to challenge entrenched norms, doctrines, and beliefs.

The freedom to criticize existing policies or governments, to call for changes in policies and governments, and to express support for unpopular political, religious, or social ideas is at the core of freedom of expression. These are precisely the exercises of expression most in need of protection. The proposed information crimes law could criminalize many forms of political, religious, and social advocacy, speech, and expression, and thus plainly infringes upon the essence of freedom of expression.

Indications of Potential Abuses

Concerns that Iraqi officials would use the law to suppress legitimate and essential kinds of expression are based on recent and current government behavior. Over the past few years, officials have filed legal actions against journalists who have published articles critical of certain officials or practices, such as articles criticizing alleged nepotism in the prime minister's office and perceived autocratic practices in the Iraqi government. And in early February 2012, the parliamentarian Haider al-Mulla reported that prosecutors were seeking to charge him with insulting Iraq's judiciary for questioning its independence from the government of Prime Minister [Nouri] al-Maliki. Given the willingness of officials to use defamation suits and even the threat of prosecution to intimidate and threaten those who peacefully challenge or criticize them, there is good reason for concern that the proposed information crimes law would add to the restrictive environment surrounding the freedom of expression in Iraq, and further deter Iraqis from exercising that right. . . .

Violations of the Right to Freedom of Association

Article 3 of the proposed information crimes law provides for life imprisonment for those who use computers and have dealings of almost any sort with any "hostile entity" for the purpose of "upsetting security and public order or endangering the country." This provision could be the basis for prosecuting anyone who has any involvement with an organization or movement that, because it is critical of the government or government policies, is deemed "hostile." Officials may regard nearly any organization, including opposition political parties, as "hostile."

Concerns that Iraqi officials would use the law to suppress freedom of association are justified because of ongoing repressive acts by the Iraqi authorities to stifle dissent.

Other provisions of the proposed law, including the provisions prohibiting the use of computers to undermine the unity of Iraq, to undermine Iraq's political or economic interests, or to inflame sectarian tensions, could also be used to target organizations and their members, and would infringe on the right to freedom of association to the extent that mere participation (involving the use of a computer or information network, which is becoming increasingly common to both formal and informal organizations) in the targeted organizations would be considered a violation of such provisions.

Therefore, the proposed law could readily be used to imprison the members of any association of which any given government disapproved and effectively ban such association. Given this, and for the reasons discussed in the previous section, (a) the law is too broad and vague to qualify, under either the ICCPR or the Iraqi Constitution, as a law that properly provides for a restriction of the freedom of association; (b) the law is not a "necessary" restriction of the freedom of association under international law; and (c) the law infringes on the "essence" of Iraqis' freedom of association.

Indications of Potential Abuse

Concerns that Iraqi officials would use the law to suppress freedom of association are justified because of ongoing repressive acts by the Iraqi authorities to stifle dissent, including attacks against NGOs [nongovernmental organizations] and political organizations. On March 6, 2011, security forces controlled by Prime Minister al-Maliki ordered [two political parties] to shut their offices after the two political parties led demonstrations in Baghdad. In April, security forces arrested without warrants three activists working for the Federation of Workers Councils and Unions for their involvement in the protests. A year later, one of the activists is still reported as missing. On May 28, 2011, soldiers raided the Baghdad office of the nongovernmental organization Ayna Haqqi ("Where Is My Right") and arrested 11 of the group's activists without a warrant. Four were released the next day; the remaining seven were detained until June 3.

Weak Ukrainian Laws Allow Cybercrime to Proliferate

Yuriy Onyshkiv

Yuriy Onyshkiv is a staff writer for the Kyiv Post. *In the following viewpoint, he reports that Ukraine's crackdown on Internet cybercrime has stalled. While two major hackers were arrested, he says, they have now been released pending trial, and in the meantime Ukraine remains a center of international cybercrime. Onyshkiv says that Ukrainian laws are inadequate for the prosecution of cybercrime. He also says that Ukraine's weak labor market has meant that those with computer skills have few legal options for employment, and so turn to cybercrime.*

As you read, consider the following questions:

1. According to Onyshkiv, who were the two Ukrainians arrested, and of what are they accused?

2. Besides the difficulty in prosecution, what does Onyshkiv say is another sign of Ukraine's weakness and vulnerability to cyber attacks?

3. Why do Internet providers have no incentive to fight spam and malware, according to Onyshkiv?

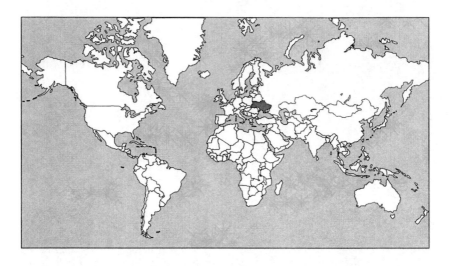

When Ukraine in October 2010 arrested five alleged hacker kingpins behind a multimillion-dollar scam, authorities touted it as part of a broader crackdown on cybercrime.

Failed Crackdown

But they were swiftly released and remain free as the investigation drags on. With more than a year passing by, Ukraine's would-be major crackdown on cybercrime is increasingly looking like the real bust.

Authorities finally admit that Ukraine remains a heavenly haven for hackers due to inadequate anti-cybercrime laws and the lack of knowledgeable computer scientists working on the side of the law.

"Ukrainian hackers are well known in the world. Our country is a potential source of cyber threats to other countries," said Valentyn Petrov, an information security official at the Security Service of Ukraine, known by its SBU acronym, on Feb. 29 [2012].

The sentencing of two convicted cyber crooks by a British court last November to four and a half years in prison each for siphoning around $4.5 million from British bank accounts only backed up this thesis.

The two Ukrainians—Yuriy Konovalenko, 29, and Yevhen Kulibaba, 33—used a computer virus to obtain confidential bank account information, which they used to transfer large sums of money from these accounts to the ones controlled by their group.

The duo pleaded guilty to conspiracy with the intent to defraud, but denied money-laundering charges. Another 11 members of the group were also sent to prison for online fraud by British courts.

It did not take British investigators very long to take the online theft case, which had been taking place between September 2009 and March 2010, to the court. In Ukraine, however, such criminals are rarely brought to justice, let alone properly prosecuted and convicted of online scams. Reports of cybercrimes originating on Ukrainian soil are numerous.

In October 2010, the SBU along with colleagues from the U.S., UK and the Netherlands claimed to have caught five members of a criminal group engaged in cybercrime. Using computer viruses they allegedly pumped $70 million from the U.S. bank accounts with more than half of the sum going to Ukrainian hackers.

Investigators say that the suspects were charged with unauthorized interference into computer networks and dissemination of malware [software that performs unauthorized actions when downloaded]. If found guilty, the accused face up to six years in prison.

The overall result depends on how successfully the Ukrainian justice system will prosecute the suspects in court.

But within a matter of months after being detained, the suspects were released by Ukrainian authorities amidst a pending investigation. Analysts describe it as yet another sign that no real crackdown is under way. Officials blame imperfect legislation and lack of authority for law enforcement.

An SBU spokeswoman excluded the possibility that the five suspects suspected of million-dollar cybercrimes could sneak out of Ukraine using fake passports. They are being closely watched, the spokesperson added.

America's FBI [Federal Bureau of Investigation] law enforcement agency originally worked with Ukraine on some of the cases and praised the crackdown. FBI officials did not, however, respond to recent inquiries asking to assess Ukraine's success on fighting Internet thefts.

Hardest Work Ahead

Computer security analysts initially also praised the success of the SBU, but noted that the hardest work is still ahead. "The overall result depends on how successfully the Ukrainian justice system will prosecute the suspects in court," said Don Jackson from [Dell] SecureWorks, a firm involved with Internet security.

Another sign of Ukraine's weakness and vulnerability to cyber attacks was obvious earlier last February when governmental websites, including SBU's web portal, were going down one by one after the temporary shutdown of EX.ua, a popular Ukrainian file-sharing website on allegations of copyright violations.

According to a written response from the interior ministry, over the last 10 years 400 people in Ukraine were detained on Internet and banking fraud charges and only eight people among them were convicted to prison sentences.

Outdated Legislation

Ukraine has frequently been cited in recent years as an origination point for cybercrimes. Analysts contend that the country is ahead of Russia as a source of spam and malware.

The Ukrainian Antivirus Scam

In March 2009, the computer security company Finjan issued a report on its investigation of an online fraud operation based in the Ukraine. The Ukrainian fraudsters implemented a scheme that was simple and ingenious: They hired rogue technical experts to inject specific, carefully chosen key words into hundreds of legitimate news and shopping websites. . . .

Once seeded into a website, the key words were picked up and indexed by search engines such as Google, which meant the search engines sent people to the altered websites. When someone's browser took him or her to one of the altered websites, scripts the experts had embedded into the altered web pages sent him or her to an external site that sold fake antivirus software. When the victim arrived at that site, a barrage of pop-up messages appeared, warning that his computer was infected with viruses and other malware [software designed to damage a computer]. The messages told the victims they needed the antivirus software being sold on the site to eliminate the infection. The antivirus software, of course, was worthless; it could not have removed any malware that might have been on a purchaser's computer.

The Finjan researchers surreptitiously monitored the scam for 16 days. During that period, more than 1.8 million people were redirected to the fake antivirus site, and 7–12 percent of them bought the fake software, which sold for $20 to $50. According to the Finjan report, if these returns were extrapolated "'[b]ased on a normal workweek, this would put [the operators of the scam] in the $2 million-plus annual income bracket.'"

Susan W. Brenner,
Cybercrime: Criminal Threats from Cyberspace.
Santa Barbara, CA: Greenwood, 2010, pp. 126–127.

"Ukraine's a huge problem. I would rank it above Russia right now," said Paul Ferguson, a researcher with Trend Micro, one of the world's top Internet security software firms.

"From what I saw, Ukraine is one of the largest centers of cybercrime," added Brian Krebs, an American computer security expert and an author of the blog *Krebs on Security*. "Not only is much of the criminal network located here, but also considerable flows of dollars obtained by hacking go here."

It was only recently that government officials publicly recognized the need to update Soviet-aged criminal legislation in order to combat 21st-century cybercrimes more efficiently.

Analysts suspect that some hackers work in Ukraine's top Internet service providers. Internet providers have no vested interest in fighting spam messages full of ads and malware. Doing so will decrease a large share of their traffic, and, in turn, income.

Petrov from Ukraine's security service believes that providers and the government have to "find a balance of interests" in this respect. Krebs says weak laws and ineffective law enforcement are to blame for poor persecution of cybercriminals.

"From a number of sources in law enforcement, I know that Ukraine has no shortage of people who want to put cybercriminals behind bars and clean up Ukraine's image as a cybercrime heaven," Krebs said. "However, if this is not combined with a competent and responsible legislative system, the rest does not matter."

It was only recently that government officials publicly recognized the need to update Soviet-aged criminal legislation in order to combat 21st-century cybercrimes more efficiently.

Petrov said Ukraine should adopt a strategy on cybersecurity and implement the Convention on Cybercrime, which was ratified by the Ukrainian parliament in 2005. The convention is the first international treaty on crimes through the Internet and aims at harmonizing international and national legislation in the field. It also provides criminal procedural tools to better investigate and prosecute such offenses.

In addition, highly skilled and educated computer programmers and engineers that do not find a developed labor market here seem to end up in lucrative unlawful business with pleasure. "There is no Eastern European Silicon Valley which would compete with the state over qualified experts in computer security," Krebs said.

Another barrier that limits access of skilled Ukrainian computer engineers to the advanced Western labor market is English language proficiency, Krebs suggests.

This is reminiscent of the turbulent 1990s post-Soviet years when former athletes, sometimes even champions, after finishing their career in sports and in search of decent salaries often joined organized crime gangs.

Weak Laws in Nigeria Allow Cybercrime to Proliferate

David Ashaolu

David Ashaolu is a principal partner at Velma Solicitors and Velma Consulting and Professional Services. In the following viewpoint, he says that the prosecution of cybercrimes in Nigeria is seriously hampered by inadequate laws. In particular, Nigerian law in many cases requires live witness testimony, which may be impossible in cybercrime cases where crimes are committed across international boundaries. Ashaolu says that there are similar problems with introducing documentary evidence into court. As a result of such limitations, Nigeria has great difficulty prosecuting cybercrimes. Ashaolu concludes that new legislation is needed to address these problems.

As you read, consider the following questions:

1. What does section 36(12) of the 1999 Nigerian Constitution state?

2. Why does Ashaolu say that the Criminal Justice (Miscellaneous Provisions) Act is obsolete and toothless?

3. According to Ashaolu, how is a document defined for legal purposes in England?

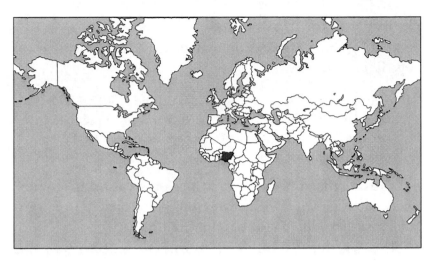

The legal regime of a phenomenon can be traced to two broad branches: the legislature and the judiciary. Perhaps, a third arm is the institutional framework which is the implementing agency that enforces the policies made by various authorities.

Suffice to point out at this juncture that Nigeria is yet to have an ICT [information, communication, and technology] law which would criminalize unlawful acts committed via and with the aid of . . . computers or computer networks. Since cybercrime is by nature committed on the cyberspace, a direct enactment prohibiting cybercrime in its intrinsic original cyber nature is *nullus secondus* [second to none] in this combat.

It will be pretentious to assume that with the few prosecutions and convictions filtering in by the day, we are achieving much in our fight against cybercrimes. When compared with what obtains in other countries around the world (even in Ghana, an African country with an ICT law), we see we are nowhere near where we should be. Certain factors which hamper the prosecution of cybercrime in Nigeria are examined hereunder.

Administrative Predicament

Section 36(12), 1999 Constitution of the Federal Republic of Nigeria provides thus:

> "a person shall not be convicted of a criminal offence unless that offence is defined and the penalty thereof prescribed in a written law; and a written law refers to an Act of the National Assembly or a law of a State"

Thus, the factors involved in the prosecution of a crime under the Nigerian law emanate from one major source: legislation. An uncodified crime is not punishable.

This position has enjoyed tremendous support from the courts over the years. In *Udokwu v Onugha*, the act complained of was committed 6 months before they were prohibited by legislation. The court held that the accused had committed no offence by virtue of Section 22(10), 1963 Constitution.

In prosecuting cybercrimes, the acts complained of must have been defined as criminal and punishable by a law of the land. Prosecuting an accused person for acts which, though we all know are wrong and unacceptable, are not criminalized by local enactments, will be tantamount to a breach of the fundamental right to fair hearing of the person so tried. Such a scenario, we are sure, will not be allowed to flourish under the present democratic dispensation of the rule of law and due process as we have it in Nigeria.

The major setback to the prosecution of all forms of cybercrimes is the lack of a direct legislation prohibiting these acts. At present, they are sociologically perceived as social vices and morally condemned as wrongs. An ICT law is the very first step towards ensuring a crime-free ICT world.

Sometime in 2004, the Nigerian Cybercrime Working Group (NCWG) was set up. The NCWG was charged with the duty of producing a cybercrime bill, an ICT law for Nigeria. But its members spent more resources on "resource control" than "crime control". Instead of setting out to work with the rigour and gusto their terms of reference required, they spent precious time clarifying who had more powers than whom. The NITDA [National Information Technology Development Agency] claimed that the cybercrime agency should be instituted under it while the EFCC [Economic and Financial Crimes Commission] wanted the agency to be integrated into its commission. The Nigerian Computer Society was advocating for a fresh independent body altogether as the cybercrime agency. That was how seven precious years have passed us by with no meaningful progress.

As a result, law enforcement agencies have been condemned to prosecuting cybercrimes by the repertoire of traditional crime legislations. For example, a crime like cyber fraud can be prosecuted under the Advance Fee Fraud and Other Related Offences Act 1995 or the offence of obtaining by false pretences under the criminal code.

Abuse of privacy, plagiarism, piracy and other intellectual property crimes committed on the Internet would have been perfectly prosecuted under a data protection act. The Nigerian Copyright Act protects intellectual property, but the definition of property does not include data stored on the computer system or certain types of software which only exist on the ICT world.

These traditional provisions are inadequate in sufficiently catering for all forms of cybercrimes, owing to the latter's inventiveness and cyber nature, characterised by cyber anonymity and pseudo-identity.

It is worth mentioning here that a Nigerian Cybersecurity Bill 2011 is currently being prepared and may be sent to the Senate soon. When this law becomes enacted, we may be singing a different tune as regards the legal regime of cybercrimes in Nigeria. But for now, law enforcement agents make do with traditional criminal law enactments to prosecute cybercrimes wherever the acts intersect. Save a special cybercrime procedural law, the existing criminal law procedural practices shall apply at the moment to these prosecutions.

Procedural Predicament

On certain occasions, however, the acts complained of may come within the ambit of the traditional legislations. . . . Where this happens, the law enforcement has in its hands an accusatorial tool for bringing cybercriminals to book. And on lesser occasions, they have secured very highly priced convictions.

The reason the convictions are not coming in as much as trials are executed is the backward state of our criminal justice system in Nigeria. The two legislations which are responsible for that aspect of our law are the Criminal Procedure Act [CPA] and the Evidence Act.

Cybercrime offences are trans-border and the needed witness . . . may not be in Nigeria to attend the proceedings. Upon that ground, the accused may be acquitted for failure to establish a prima facie *case against him.*

The [Criminal Procedure] Act was enacted June 1, 1945, scores of years before the Internet came into Nigeria and decades of years before the Internet was even invented. It makes provisions for the mode of prosecuting criminals including certain fundamental issues like jurisdiction, examination of witnesses and admissibility of evidence. Unfortunately, however, the CPA was not enacted with ICT in mind. This is understandable as cyberspace was still in oblivion at the time it was codified.

Under the CPA, witnesses are expected to be physically present in court during trials. In fact, any witness who fails to appear personally could be summoned (subpoenaed) and detained and may be released on bail upon the same bail conditions available to the accused person. Even children, infants and young persons (below 17 years) who may need to give evidences in court in camera for security and other reasons still have to be physically present or their testimonies would not be accepted.

Cybercrime offences are trans-border and the needed witness who would give the very material evidence may not be in Nigeria to attend the proceedings. Upon that ground, the accused may be acquitted for failure to establish a *prima facie* [at first sight] case against him by reason of insufficient evidence. He may also be discharged for want of diligent prosecution. This was not envisaged by the drafters of the act.

This position is contrary to what obtains in England, for example. The Criminal Justice Act 1988 made an important provision for the admission of video recordings of interview with child witnesses carried out before the trial. By Section 28(1) of the same act, cross-examinations and re-examinations can be recorded and televised in court. . . .

Criminal Justice (Miscellaneous Provisions) Act

This [the Criminal Justice (Miscellaneous Provisions) Act] is an addendum to the criminal code and the Criminal Procedure Act. It is an act to impose "stiffer penalties" on persons who damage, disrupt or destroy telecommunications, electrical transmission lines and oil pipelines. The provisions as they relate to cybercrimes are examined hereunder.

"Any person who . . . prevents or obstructs the sending or delivering of communications by means of telecommunications . . . is guilty of an offence." The penalty is a fine of N500 [about 3 US dollars] or 3 years' imprisonment or both. Thus, hacking, where interception is occasioned, can come under this heading, since a hacker uses the telecoms. This will also sufficiently cover offences like illegal interception.

Section 9 defines telephone works as meaning wire or wires used for telegram and telecommunications, with any

Top Ten Countries by Counts of Cybercrime Perpetrated, 2009

1. United States	65.4%
2. United Kingdom	9.9%
3. Nigeria	8.0%
4. Canada	2.6%
5. Malaysia	0.7%
6. Ghana	0.7%
7. South Africa	0.7%
8. Spain	0.7%
9. Cameroon	0.6%
10. Australia	0.5%

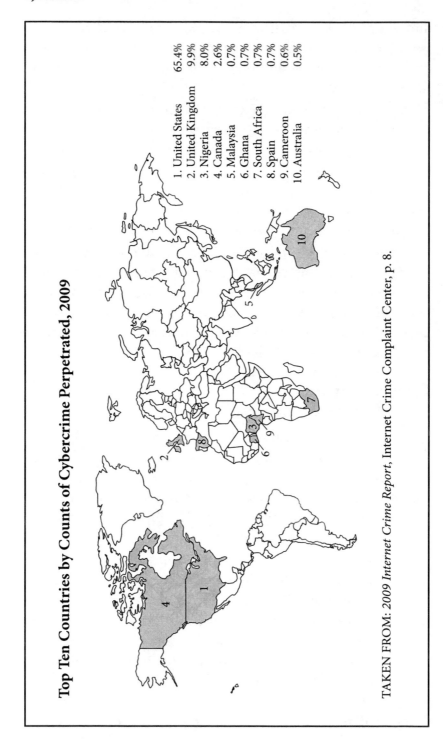

TAKEN FROM: *2009 Internet Crime Report*, Internet Crime Complaint Center, p. 8.

casing, coating, tube, pipe, insulator, etc. and including any apparatus for transmitting messages or other matters including the television, by means of electronic signals whether by overhead lines or underground cables or cables lying under water and any apparatus for transmitting messages with or without wires.

It is very clear from the wordings of the act that a computer system was not in the contemplation of the drafters of this law, neither was the Internet. The consistent mentioning of cables and wires and other physical equipments, specifically the express mention of a television shows that the cyberspace was unknown to the act that was drafted October 16, 1975—two decades before the first ISP [Internet service provider] licence was issued in Nigeria. From the wordings of the act, it is deductible that its aim is to protect government appliances and equipment and other public property from sabotage, damage and theft.

Another inadequacy in the act is with the provision of Section 7(1) and (2) which puts prosecution at the instance of the attorney general of the federation. With that office being more politically concerned than it is with the administration of justice, prosecution may never happen. Also, the hilarious fine of N500 [about 3 US dollars] makes it seem to us like this obsolete law is more of a toothless dog, whose bark is worse than its bite.

Evidence Act

The Evidence Act was first enacted by an ordinance in 1943. . . . [It was amended in 2011.]

Generally, there are 3 methods of tendering evidence to prove facts in the court of law under the Evidence Act. We have the direct oral evidence, the documentary evidence and the visitation to the *locus in quo* [scene of the event].

Oral Evidence

By Sections 125 & 126, all facts, except the contents of a document, may be proved by oral evidence which must be direct in all cases. The act defines the adjective 'direct' to include anything, state of things, or relation of things, capable of being perceived by the senses, or any mental condition of which any person is conscious. This means that an oral evidence of a fact will not be admissible in the court if it is not given by a witness who came in contact with such fact in a manner consistent with the 5 human senses, viz the eyes, mouth, irritation, taste and smell. Direct oral evidence therefore requires a witness to be physically present in court and 'sensually' relate the version of the facts that he has personally come within the knowledge of, or is 'conscious' of.

Although the 2011 Evidence Act makes room for the admissibility of computer-generated and electronic evidence, it sufficiently excludes applying such technology to the tendering of oral evidence.

However, in other jurisdictions with improved criminal justice systems and procedural laws, the sensual requirement has been jettisoned. The use of technology like visual displays is now employed in the courtrooms to provide evidence in trials. These visual displays are computer generated. Other times, the witnesses are video recorded and subsequently broadcast in the court. According to [Declan] O'Flaherty, this method of evidence gives the court the advantages of stop action, varied perspective and slow motion. It is also possible to enlarge, highlight, duplicate and compare evidences.

This has made the reception of the testimonies of experts like doctors and engineers via online video conferencing link possible. Also, it has been shown that documents can be presented on screen in their unaltered form and in a way that they can be inspected, enlarged or otherwise electronically enhanced. As mentioned above, evidences of certain witnesses are also recorded and replayed in the courtroom.

Although the 2011 Evidence Act makes room for the admissibility of computer-generated and electronic evidence, it sufficiently excludes applying such technology to the tendering of oral evidence. The reference to electronic production of evidence and computer-generated evidence is restricted to documents, including such analogous facts like maps and graphs.

Documentary Evidence

Unlike the restrictive definition of a document under the old Evidence Act, the new law defines a document to technically include virtually every tangible thing from paper to a video recording, capable of storing or recording information. In particular, paragraph (d) of the Section 258 defines a document as "any device by means of which information is recorded, stored or retrievable, including computer output." This is perhaps the whole essence of the amendment, as a reaction to the highly limiting provisions of the now extinct 2004 Evidence Act, which would not even recognise a document printed from a computer.

The bulk of correspondences and exchanges of information involved in the perpetration of cybercrimes is done via e-mail.

This is in consonance with the growing trend of documentary evidence the world over, especially in other jurisdictions like England, where the reach of the concept of a document has been extended, giving it its widest possible meaning. A document is defined simply—yet technically—as anything in which information of any description is recorded.

With this provision, the judgment of Muntaka-Coomaise JCA in the case of *UBA v. Sani Abacha Foundation* is no longer the law in Nigeria. . . .

E-mail

Let us consider e-mail, for instance. An e-mail is an electronic message sent in cyberspace. One characteristic of the e-mail that makes it a juicy subject is the speed by which it is delivered and its ability to be delivered on almost any device. It can be delivered to several people all over the world simultaneously while the sender still keeps his exact copy of the mail he sent without losing value, content or quantity. Also, it is totally oblivious of geographical divides and is stored on a third-party server, thereby making it available for use anywhere in the world upon a successful access of the third-party mail server, without requiring the user to keep a personal copy. The third-party mail server assigns to everyone on its system a specific volume of storage space. E-mails are usually saved in a folder called 'Inbox', except where specific filtering rules have been applied. Apart from containing messages which would otherwise have been written in a traditional letter, it can also contain attachments like other files and documents, pictures, sounds, videos, and so on. . . .

Highly incriminating facts can be contained in an e-mail. In fact, the bulk of correspondences and exchanges of information involved in the perpetration of cybercrimes is done via e-mail. An e-mail sent as a correspondence from Puerto Rico will be readable in my inbox anywhere I am in the world, regardless of where I was when the e-mail was sent, and for a lifetime. And except [when] I delete it, I can use the mail here in the United States and use the same mail when I get to Lagos, Nigeria. It is therefore difficult to determine at every material point under whose jurisdiction the e-mail was, or where exactly it can be located. Unlike a folder in a generic computer which can be traced to a path or directory, the e-mail folder is an intangible entity with no geographical location. Its existence is spatial. Yet, tons of materials, information as well as evidences can be safely tucked away in this cloud safe.

Other types of computer-produced documents that will most likely be needed in proving a cybercrime include contents on a website hosted on the Internet. In this situation, the contents are stored on the computer system of the owner (or host, depending) of the website who may be in India or Sweden, but is visible and available to everyone everywhere in the world. To obtain such a document, secondary methods will be adopted like saving and printing the image of the website, copying its content and pasting it in another programme in order to get a copy suitable for trial, and so on. Here again, it is difficult to guarantee its sanctity, as it has been subject to manipulations.

Having identified the various types of documents that may pop up in a cybercrime trial (while not pretending to have provided an exhaustive list), I shall next examine what the act says about computer-obtained evidence.

Section 84 of the act provides that, provided it can be established that the document sought to be tendered was produced by the computer from information supplied to it during a period over which the computer was used regularly and functioning properly to store and process information for the purpose for which that document was produced at that particular time, any statement contained in such document shall be admissible as evidence of any fact stated in it of which direct oral evidence would be admissible, in any proceedings.

This provision clearly excludes documents subsequently edited after it had been earlier produced and stored in a period in which the computer was used for the purpose of its production. It must also be shown that the information contained in the statement reproduces or is derived from information supplied to the computer in the ordinary course of those activities and at that particular period.

By Section 84(3), where more than one computer is involved in the process of producing the document, all the computers shall be regarded as one computer for the purpose of the production of the said document. Thus, in line with the provision of the act dealing with primary evidence of a document, any part of the document produced from any of these computers shall be deemed to be primary evidence of the said document and shall be admissible accordingly.

The drafters of the act envisaged the possibility of some of the issues raised earlier in this [viewpoint] as it relates to computer-produced documents. To ameliorate this situation, subsection 4 of the same section provides that a person occupying a responsible position in relation to the operation of the computer or relevant device or the management of the relevant activities shall tender a certificate. The certificate, which minimally shall be to the best of his knowledge and belief, may identify the document containing the statement, describe the manner in which it was produced, give the particulars of the device involved in the production of that document in order to show that the document was produced by a computer or establish that the document was produced in the period and for the purpose for which the document was originally produced. . . .

How do we ask our judges to visit the cyberspace? Where is it located?

From the foregoing, the act seems to have sufficiently catered for documents produced by or through a computer system, manned by "a person occupying a responsible position" in relation to the operation of the computer or the management of relevant activities at the time of its production, who would be able to make a certificate. But the inadequacy of these provisions still abound where the document is stored on the cyberspace. Of course, access to such a document becomes a major primary concern, especially where it is a private document like an e-mail which the state may not access without the consent of the accused person. In any case, where an online document (like website contents) has been produced or obtained by a computer, how do we identify such an appropriate officer versed enough with the knowledge of the facts to present such a required certificate? It is sadly submitted that the act missed a golden opportunity to make our evidence law information technology compliant.

Visit to the *locus in quo*

Visit to the *locus in quo* means the court may, at certain times as necessary, visit the scene of a crime to get the real evidence and inspect the spot of the crime. At times, the court may continue the proceedings at the *locus*. At other times, it may only adjourn and recommence proceedings after it had visited the *locus*. The accused person must however be there at the visitation.

How do we ask our judges to visit the cyberspace? Where is it located? The only means of achieving such an aim in a cybercrime trial is to bring to the courtroom, evidence lifted off the Internet via the computer. This procedure will include the taking of oral evidence of witnesses, some of whom may not be able to come to Nigeria but may be able to provide his testimony through online video conferencing, VoIP [voice over Internet Protocol] services like Skype, live video streaming of the proceedings, and so on. It will also include the need for the judge to access the computer systems or go online himself and confirm some of the facts presented, whenever that may become necessary. Further, documents which exist in the cyberspace may be needed in further proving these cases.

But since our Evidence Act is shortsighted enough not to accommodate these specific cyber-related evidence procedures, law enforcement agents meet a brick wall in prosecuting cybercriminals.

Even our latest attempt at amending our Evidence Act and enacting a new one does not solve the cyber-related shortcomings of our criminal law. . . .

It is here submitted that time is ripe for Nigeria to have an information and communications technology law that will combat cybercrimes headlong. Such a provision, like the Indian Information Technology Law 2000, would make provisions for both the procedural and the substantive aspects of cybercrimes in particular and cyber law in general. As we progress to the new year, our hopes are high for the proposed Nigerian cybersecurity bill currently being prepared.

In Australia, Combating Cybercrime Should Begin by Supporting and Funding Existing Organizations

Stilgherrian

Stilgherrian is a writer, broadcaster, and consultant based in Sydney, Australia. In the following viewpoint, he responds to recommendations for new regulations and new governmental bodies and committees to fight cybercrime in Australia. He argues that Australia already has institutions designed to fight crime—specifically, the police. What is needed, he says, is not more agencies, but more resources and training for the agency that is already charged with fighting crime of all sorts, whether on the Internet or elsewhere.

As you read, consider the following questions:

1. What statements from the report he discusses does Stilgherrian single out as naïve?
2. Why does Stilgherrian say that the ACMA would not do a good job of combating a malware outbreak?
3. According to Stilgherrian, what is one bright spot in the report he discusses?

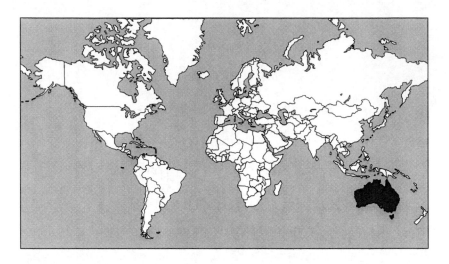

N^o wonder the cyber criminals are winning.

Naïve Politicians

If the inquiry into cyber crime report is a true indication of our federal parliament's understanding of this issue, it's no wonder the bad guys are winning.

This by no means reflects poorly on the staffers who prepared "Hackers, Fraudsters and Botnets: Tackling the Problem of Cyber Crime" released Monday [June 2010]. Their terms of reference have been fulfilled, and indeed they've produced a perfectly good summary of the state of cyber crime and Australia's ability to deal with it. Nor does it reflect poorly on the committee's good intentions.

No, the problem is that the politicians are still way behind the pace, as they always seem to be when it comes to the Internet. As a result, the report starts at the very, very beginning and makes naïve recommendations.

"The Internet has ... become a critical part of the communications infrastructure of most modern economies," begins the report's introduction. Who knew? "Financial gain was repeatedly identified as the prime motivator of cybercrime," it says later. As opposed to other kinds of organized crime, presumably, which are motivated by a love of puppies.

Stating-the-obvious aside, some of the report's recommendations are sensible enough, if long overdue. Setting up a 24/7 crime-reporting hotline with no minimum crime value. Strategically targeting the black markets in malicious software tools and personal information. Disrupting the botnets of hacked computers that now provide the infrastructure for crime, and identifying and prosecuting their managers. Collecting up-to-date data and keeping parliament informed. Reviewing legislation. Signing up to the Council of Europe Convention on Cybercrime.

But some recommendations are . . . curious, to say the least.

The idea that Internet service providers (ISPs) should contractually require customers to install antivirus software and firewalls before they can connect to the Internet has received the most media attention. Security consultant Alastair MacGibbon wants to go even further, requiring ISPs to monitor customers' computers and prevent them from connecting if their security software isn't up to scratch.

On the surface it seems attractive. After all, cars have safety checks before they're allowed on the roads. Electrical appliances and telephone equipment must be approved and, at least in workplaces, subject to regular compliance testing. But this scheme would be almost impossible to implement effectively.

Other curious recommendations include creating a swathe of new agencies to coordinate the battle against cyber crime—despite such agencies already existing.

Internet-connected devices don't just include computers running Windows, Mac OS X or Linux. There's also gaming consoles, smartphones using Wi-Fi, Internet "radio" receivers, newfangled TVs with built-in YouTube and Skype, e-book readers, iPads and only the gods know how many specialist devices for professional use. In such a diverse and rapidly changing environment, who decides on the appropriate level of protection? And how do you decide whether that protection is correctly configured given users' unique needs?

I'm sure the geeks amongst you can list dozens more flaws. Off you go.

Most important of all, how does any of this defend against the majority of malicious software, which uses social engineering techniques to persuade the user to install it, technical protections or not?

Poor Recommendations

Other curious recommendations include creating a swathe of new agencies to coordinate the battle against cyber crime—despite such agencies already existing.

An office of online security headed by a cyber security co-ordinator in the Department of the Prime Minister and Cabinet? "It is not clear how this role would differ from the Internet security–related bodies already formed, or why it should be in the Prime Minister's Department, rather than one of the agencies which has expertise in the Internet security," notes ANU [Australian National University]'s Tom Worthington, a longtime observer of information security issues.

An intelligence hub to "facilitate information sharing within and across industry sectors"? But we already have Aus-CERT, the nonprofit computer emergency response team that says it'll still be operating even though there's now also CERT Australia in the Attorney-General's Department.

A National Cyber Crime Advisory Committee, *and* a national government working group on cyber crime, *and* a police "E Crime Managers Group"?

Most curious of all, there's a call for the Australian Communications and Media Authority (ACMA) to expand its collection of data on malware-infected computers into the realm of infected web pages, and that this data "be collated and provided as daily aggregated reports to Internet service providers".

A major malware outbreak can sweep the globe in 20 minutes. Is this really best handled by ACMA, operating during public service business hours and already taking 60-odd days to respond to complaints about refused classification [material blocked from the web in Australia] content?

"It is not clear why ACMA is recommended for this role, over agencies which have expertise in Internet security," Worthington writes. "The report further recommends ACMA support emergency response functions of government, although this function is already assigned to the Department of Defence in the Telecommunications Act."

Focus on Crime

The problem, I think, is that the focus is on the "cyber" rather than the "crime".

As the Australian Bureau of Statistics noted in its submission, "cyber crime is not a stand-alone criminal offence, but rather reflects a broad spectrum of criminal offence types and behaviours committed via electronic means." In many cases, they're traditional crimes that now happen to involve the Internet at some point—fraud, child exploitation, theft and blackmail.

We already have organizations dedicated to fighting crime: the police.

We don't treat "vehicle crime" separately just because a car was involved. Cyber crime should be no different.

Of course there's a skills shortage here. One bright spot is that the report recommends the development of a national law enforcement training facility for the investigation of cyber crime.

The key, I think, is not starting from scratch with another new bureaucracy. It's supporting our existing organizations, with their existing relationships, and funding them properly so that a crime is dealt with intelligently, professionally and aggressively—whether it involves a "cyber" or not.

Periodical and Internet Sources Bibliography

The following articles have been selected to supplement the diverse views presented in this chapter.

AllAfrica — "Nigeria: Growing Menace of Cybercrime," September 20, 2012. http://allafrica.com.

Taylor Armerding — "Ukraine Seen as a Growing 'Haven for Hackers,'" CSO Online, March 13, 2012. www.csoonline.com.

BBC News — "Philippine Cybercrime Law Takes Effect Amid Protests," October 3, 2012.

Sung Un Kim — "HRW: Iraq Draft Cybercrime Law Violates Free Speech," Jurist, July 12, 2012. http://jurist.org.

Michael Lee — "Cybercrime Bill Passes Senate, Set to Become Law," ZDNet.com, August 22, 2012.

Nancy Messieh — "French Advisory Council Speaks Out Against Sarkozy's Plan to Criminalize Visiting Extremist Websites," *The Next Web* (blog), March 27, 2012. http://thenextweb.com.

Danny O'Brien — "Computer Crime Laws Belie Thai Claim to Modern Society," Committee to Protect Journalists, May 31, 2012.

Danny O'Brien — "Iraqi Cybercrime Bill Is the Worst Kind," Committee to Protect Journalists, March 30, 2012.

Paul Shea — "Nicolas Sarkozy's Internet Censorship Plan Opposed by His Own Council," ValueWalk, March 27, 2012. www.valuewalk.com.

Deb Shinder — "Juvenile Cyber-Delinquency: Laws That Are Turning Kids into Criminals," *TechRepublic*, February 7, 2012. www.techrepublic.com.

GLOBALVIEWPOINTS

CHAPTER 3

Organized Crime and Cybercrime

Russian Cybercrime Thrives as Soviet-Era Schools Spawn Hackers

Anastasia Ustinova

Anastasia Ustinova is a St. Petersburg–based reporter for Bloomberg. In the following viewpoint, Ustinova reports on growing levels of cybercrime in Russia. She says that the increase is because hackers in Russia, trained in Soviet-era schools, do not have outlets for their talents. Therefore, she maintains, they become involved in cybercrime. She reports that Russia is working to create more Internet industry and online opportunities to take advantage of the computer engineering talent among young Russians.

As you read, consider the following questions:

1. According to Ustinova, who is Viktor Pleshchuk, and what did he do?
2. What does Dmitry Zakharov say that the Russian government needs to do to fight cybercrime?
3. How did hackers steal money from RBS WorldPay, according to Ustinova?

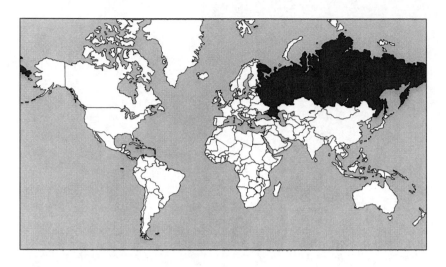

The U.S. Department of Justice said it may have been the most sophisticated computer fraud ever. For Viktor Pleshchuk, it was the chance to buy a brand new BMW and an apartment in his hometown of St. Petersburg.

The 29-year-old last month pleaded guilty to participating in a worldwide hacking scheme that led to the illegal withdrawal of more than $9 million from cash machines worldwide operated by RBS WorldPay Inc., the U.S. payment-processing division of Britain's Royal Bank of Scotland Group Plc.

The conviction shed light on a growing trend from Russia. Just as President Dmitry Medvedev seeks to persuade investors his country is a safe place, more technology graduates are turning to cybercrime. The FBI last week charged 37 suspects from Russia, Ukraine and other Eastern European countries of using a computer virus to hack into U.S. bank accounts.

"The number of hackers reflects how many good engineers we potentially have in this country," Vladimir Dolgov, the president of Google Inc. in Russia, said in a Bloomberg Television interview in Moscow.

Russians committed more than 17,500 computer-related crimes last year, or 25 percent more than in 2008, according to the interior ministry's latest statistics.

'Childish Prank'

While cybercrime is proliferating, Russian laws against it were written in 1998, when hacking was often perceived as a "childish prank," Boris Miroshnikov, the head of the ministry's anti-cybercrime department, said in a report posted on the agency's website.

A ministry spokeswoman said the department has advised Russian lawmakers to impose stiffer penalties on hackers. She declined to be identified, citing department policy.

"We are working on that, but so far we haven't moved beyond discussions," she said.

Businesses around the world lose more than $1 trillion in intellectual property due to data theft and cybercrime annually, according to a report in January 2009 by McAfee Inc., the technology security company based in Santa Clara, California.

Seeking to thwart the attacks, U.S. legislators in March proposed to use trade restrictions to penalize countries that provide safe haven to hackers.

Growing Threat

"The cybercrime threat coming from Russia is significant and growing," U.S. senator Kirsten Gillibrand, a New York Democrat who supports the measure, said in an e-mailed response to questions. "It threatens America and undermines the Russians. It is in the best interest of both countries to find a way to cooperate and better control cybercrime."

The FBI said on Sept. 30 the suspects from Eastern Europe stand accused on trying to hack into U.S. bank accounts to steal more than $3 million. In August, French authorities arrested a resident of Moscow who used his Internet network called CarderPlanet to sell stolen credit cards, the U.S. Secret Service said in a statement on its website.

"Hackers are not gangsters with knives, but young and talented kids from suburbs who don't have any other options to make a living."

"This network has been repeatedly linked to nearly every major intrusion of financial information reported to the international law enforcement community," the agency said in the statement.

The government in Moscow needs to create jobs to help thwart cyber criminals. Their numbers have swelled since the collapse of the Soviet Union, when scores of Russian computer engineers turned to online crime, Dmitry Zakharov, a spokesman at the Russian Association for Electronic Communications, said.

"Hackers are not gangsters with knives, but young and talented kids from suburbs who don't have any other options to make a living," said Zakharov. "If the government will create jobs for them, many will follow the lead."

Shy Hacker

Medvedev, 45, who has a video blog and a Twitter account, has said he wants to stop the Russian brain drain and turn the economy away from energy exports toward one based on technology.

The president asked billionaire Viktor Vekselberg in March to oversee plans to create a hub for the development and marketing of new technologies in the Moscow suburb of Skolkovo, where tax breaks and other incentives would be offered to lure investment. Companies including Siemens AG, Cisco Systems Inc. and Nokia Oyj have agreed to participate in the project.

Pleshchuk was a "positive and shy" student who "worked hard," Sergey Sharangovich, head of the department that edu-

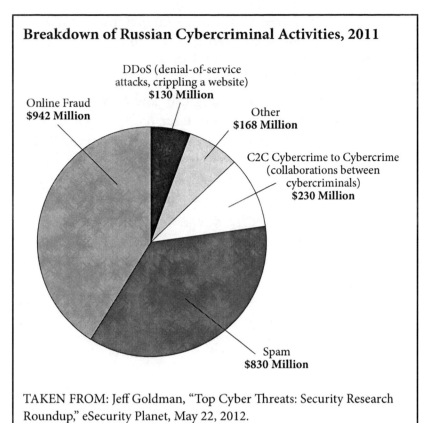

Breakdown of Russian Cybercriminal Activities, 2011

Online Fraud
$942 Million

DDoS (denial-of-service
attacks, crippling a website)
$130 Million

Other
$168 Million

C2C Cybercrime to Cybercrime
(collaborations between
cybercriminals)
$230 Million

Spam
$830 Million

TAKEN FROM: Jeff Goldman, "Top Cyber Threats: Security Research Roundup," eSecurity Planet, May 22, 2012.

cated him, said in a statement on the website of Tomsk State University of Control Systems and Radioelectronics.

After graduating, he moved to St. Petersburg and opened an e-commerce company before he got in touch with a group of international hackers who asked him to help crack WorldPay's database, Russian investigators said.

'Sophisticated'

The U.S. Justice Department last year indicted Pleshchuk and seven other hackers in Russia and elsewhere in Eastern Europe, saying the group stole the data encryption that was used by RBS WorldPay to protect debit cards, it said on its website.

The cards were used to withdraw money from 2,100 cash machines in 280 cities in less than 12 hours, in what U.S. prosecutors called "perhaps the most sophisticated and organized computer-fraud attack ever conducted."

"We take fraud extremely seriously and have stringent security processes in place to protect our customers, which we constantly review," Michael Strachan, a spokesman at RBS in London, said in an e-mailed statement.

Pleshchuk got a reduced sentence, including four years' probation, after he agreed to provide information about his accomplices, his lawyer, Yuriy Novolodsky, said in an interview in St. Petersburg last month. He was ordered to give up his assets, including the BMW and the apartment, to help pay the $9 million back to WorldPay.

"On the one hand, it's flattering," Sharangovich at Tomsk University said. "On the other hand, Pleshchuk didn't apply his knowledge the right way."

Worldwide, Cybercrime Is Committed by Organized Crime Members, Not by Hackers

John Leyden

John Leyden is a reporter for the Register, *an online technology publication. In the following viewpoint, he reports that a new study shows that most cybercriminals do not fit the stereotype of young, brilliant hackers. Instead, he says, most cybercrime is committed by organized criminal networks, usually involving older perpetrators with limited Internet or coding skills, who use off-the-shelf programs to commit their crimes. In fact, Leyden reports, cybercrime is often the offshoot of other organized criminal activity. He concludes that a better understanding of the perpetrators may help authorities reduce cybercrime.*

As you read, consider the following questions:

1. What does Leyden say has been the result of the de-skilling of cybercrime?
2. How big are cybercrime rings according to Leyden, and how does the size of the ring correlate with the scope of cybercrime offenses?

3. What does the study Leyden discusses say about the length of time that many cybercrime rings have been operational?

Assumptions about cybercriminals are all wrong, according to a study that argues many fraudsters are middle-aged and possess only rudimentary IT [information technology] skills—contrary to the elite bedroom teen hackers portrayed in movies.

Older Gangsters

The research, led by criminologist Dr Michael McGuire of the John Grieve Centre for Policing and [Community Safety] at London Metropolitan University, blames 80 per cent of cybercrime on your common or garden gangsters. Contrary to Hollywood film scripts, cybercrime is far from the preserve of tech-savvy youths—nearly half (43 per cent) of cyber crooks are over 35 years old, and less than a third (29 per cent) are under 25.

More cyber crooks (11 per cent) are over 50 than youngsters aged between 14 and 18, who make up only eight per cent of e-crims, according to the doctor and his team.

The study, sponsored by BAE [Systems] Detica, is billed as the first comprehensive analysis of the nature of criminal organisations involved in e-crime. The document could help cops tackle banking fraud and other scams more effectively by challenging existing assumptions about the cyber-crook demographic.

The availability of crime ware, which can be easily distributed or purchased, means getting ready-made viruses that exploit the vulnerabilities of individual systems to running botnets [a collection of compromised computers] of hijacked computers can be accomplished without any particular technical skills. Cyber crooks are now just as likely to be street gangs, drug traffickers or established crime families as those

Typical Ages of Organized Digital Crime Associates

Age	Percentage
14–18	8%
19–25	21%
26–35	29%
36–50	32%
50+	11%

43% are over 35 years old.

TAKEN FROM: BAE Systems Detica and the John Grieve Centre, *Organised Crime in the Digital Age: The Real Picture*, Executive Summary, 2012, p. 5.

traditionally associated with digital crime such as ID [identity] fraudsters or hacking syndicates.

The "de-skilling" of cybercrime has allowed many traditional off-line scams to be applied online. For example, money laundering has been extended to the creation of money mule networks to siphon funds from compromised web accounts, and the control of drugs markets has been applied in selling unlicensed medicines.

Growth in the digital economy will inevitably cause an increase in organised digital crime, however, this need not be seen as an insurmountable problem.

How Many Are in Your Gang?

Half the groups involved in cybercrime are made up of six individuals or more, with one-quarter comprising 11 or more. However, there's little or no correlation between group size and the impact or scope of offending.

A small group of cyber crooks can inflict huge financial harm against targeted institutions. And many cybercrime crews have been operating for months rather than years. A quarter

(25 per cent) of active groups have operated for less than six months, the *Organised Crime in the Digital Age* study concludes. The report reveals that certain clusters of criminal activity exhibit more organisation or structure than others on a spectrum that extends from decentralised swarms through to highly organised hierarchies. In some cases classic crime families that have begun to move their off-line activities into cyberspace—rubbing shoulders with extremist groups recruiting members online, and protesters coordinating riots using web tools.

Professor John Grieve, founder of the policing centre, commented:

> To tackle the problem of digital crime and intervene successfully, we need to move away from traditional models and embrace this new information about how organised criminals operate in a digital context.

> The research found evidence of many cases where there has been real success in closing down digital criminal operations. Growth in the digital economy will inevitably cause an increase in organised digital crime, however, this need not be seen as an insurmountable problem. Rather, it is a predictable problem that—by better understanding the perpetrators and their working methods—we can meet head-on.

The team of researchers who carried out the study combined seeking out information by hand with advanced search tools—such as Detica's NetReveal Analyzer, a bit of gear designed to turn large amounts of structured and unstructured data into intelligence. Stage one of the research involved a review of evidence made up of over 7,000 documentary sources, including public and private documentation to analyse the technologies, activities, group characteristics and miscreants involved in cybercrime.

Then the team performed a demographic analysis of initial organisational patterns found in these sources and compared the results with evidence from interviews with expert practitioners. Finally, a network analysis of the organisational patterns and activities that emerged at the earlier stages of the research process was carried out to arrive at the study's final conclusions.

In Mexico, Drug Cartels Are Moving into Cybercrime

Infosec Institute

The Infosec Institute is an information technology training facil-ity. In the following viewpoint, the author reports that drug car-tels in Mexico are moving into cybercriminal activities such as hacking into bank systems and perpetrating credit card fraud scams. To help them in these activities, the author says, the car-tels will kidnap hackers. In addition, the cartels have been tar-geting individuals who report on their activities using social me-dia. The cartels, the author reports, have already largely silenced regular media with threats and are now moving to intimidate individuals discussing the drug war on Twitter, Facebook, or other social media platforms.

As you read, consider the following questions:

1. What is Anonymous, and how and why did it threaten the Los Zetas cartel, according to the author?
2. What action by the cartels does the author say caused the escalation of social media reports on the gangs?
3. What two incidents in September 2011 does the author say marked the initial cartel counteroffensive against social media?

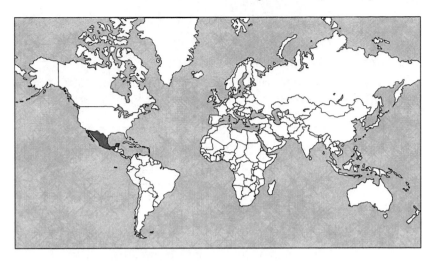

Mexican drug trafficking organizations are increasingly demonstrating a desire to make money from cyber crime, attracted by the high profits and minimal risks, offered by such activities as fraud, theft, and piracy.

Kidnapping Hackers

These gangs lack the needed technical know-how within their ranks, which means they would be desperate to recruit programmers with the expertise to break into the world of cyber crime.

Recent claims that computer programmers are being forcibly recruited by Mexican drug gangs, if true, suggest that these groups are acquiring the ability to reap the potential profits of cyber crime.

It has emerged that computer and IT [information technology] experts have been hacking into bank systems and program credit card fraud scams, among other activities, in order to acquire additional funds for the cartels, on top of what they already get from selling drugs.

According to specialists, the potential profits generated from this kind of criminal activity is already comparable to that coming from the drugs.

Dmitry Bestuzhev, a specialist with Kaspersky Lab, stated that attacks on the world's largest banks in the US, Europe or Russia are taking place on a daily basis.

It is expected that we'll be seeing these hacker kidnappings much more often.

As mainstream media go quiet, scared citizens turned to online sources for clues about how to stay safe.

Anonymous vs. Los Zetas

In October 2011 the hacker group Anonymous, responsible for breaching the security of banks, financial institutions and government agencies, threatened Los Zetas, a Mexican drug cartel and a former paramilitary-wing of the Gulf Cartel, for kidnapping one of its members from a street protest in the Mexican state of Veracruz.

The threat was issued via an online video and a 5 November [2012] ultimatum was given to Los Zetas.

If the member was not released, Anonymous said it would start hacking into secure websites/protected accounts and release sensitive information concerning the members of Los Zetas and those working with them, such as journalists and police officers.

They stated that they were prepared to hack into cartel members' bank accounts and wreak financial havoc on the drug dealers.

According to the *Long War Journal*, [it] is possible that Anonymous came into this conflict due to the cartel policy of torturing and killing Mexican bloggers.

A member of Anonymous said that they went after the Zetas only because of the kidnapping of its member and that the group's real target was the Mexican government.

According to security experts, releasing information on Los Zetas collaborators, hacked from police data banks, would likely put the suspects on a "kill list" of rival cartels.

When the kidnapped activist was freed on the 4th of November, with a note from her captors threatening to kill 10 people for every name that became public, the all Anonymous Operation—OpCartel—was called off.

Anonymous members involved in OpCartel say they're not giving up the fight, only changing targets. Anonymous apparently abandoned their plans to take on the Zetas cartel.

Mexican Citizens Turn to Social Networks

After a long campaign of intimidation and murder that produced 74 Mexican journalists killed since 2000, many traditional media outlets have stopped reporting on drug-related crime. Mexican newspapers and other media have been self-censoring themselves after drug cartels began targeting them for reporting on the gangs.

As a result, the use of social media exploded across Mexico, online activists are filling the vacuum. As mainstream media go quiet, scared citizens turned to online sources for clues about how to stay safe.

Concerned Mexican citizens established social media networks—derived from courageous news websites, such as *Blog del Narco* and *Frontera al Rojo Vivo*, texting and tweeting, trying to bypass the cartel assault on press freedoms in Mexico.

They have taken to Facebook, Twitter, and forums just to communicate basic information they need to survive day to day, since visible and known television, radio, and newspaper reporters won't cover these stories for fear of their own lives.

These citizens share information like where the cartels have struck, what has it done to traffic or is it safe to walk my children down the street without seeing another cartel's victim hanging off the overpass.

This escalation of social media came months after Los Zetas launched a series of YouTube videos, in the summer of

2011, threatening people in Veracruz warning them against using social media to provide information to the authorities and law enforcement.

Those threats enraged Mexican youth, who took up the threat as a challenge—and soon, Facebook and Twitter were full with leads about the narcos.

In Mexican cities, Twitter and Facebook started serving as platforms for crowd-sourced intelligence on the drug gangs. Blogs replaced newspapers as sources.

Online offerings include official anonymous tip sites, specialist blogs which carry explicit photos of cartel murder victims and neighborhood watch–style sites.

Hashtags—which tie Twitter posts together—have become an important sorting mechanism, turning connected reports by individual Twitter accounts into ad hoc news services. For instance, in Tamaulipas state, Twitter users developed codes to indicate the level of confidence about information posted.

Twitter is indispensable for obtaining real-time information from within Mexico and along the border as events unfold. Twitter is extremely useful especially when authorities and media don't want to report the events.

Over time, users have grown more daring. The editors at *Nuevo Laredo en Vivo* compiled reports to create a map of drug sale locations and suspected lookouts.

In fact, it's not unusual for online activists to battle the drug cartels. *Blog del Narco* was one of the first, documenting the comings and goings of members and supporters of the Sinaloa drug cartel.

However, reports of violence which are based solely on social media also open the door for unconfirmed rumors to spread quickly.

In Veracruz, a man and a woman were charged with terrorism and sabotage after passing along rumors of an impending drug cartel attack on a school, using Twitter.

Journalists and the Cartels

The story of the rise of El Narco [Mexico's drug cartels] is also the story of Mexican journalists who risk their lives to cover it. The American and British press could get nowhere with their special features of Pulitzer Prize pieces on Mexico without building on the work done day in, day out by Mexican reporters, photographers, and cameramen up and down the country. The grunts' digging and muckraking has even been the main source of investigations by Mexican police and American agents. For salaries as low as $400 a month, reporters resist attacks and intimidation to expose corruption and search for justice.

Of course, the story of Mexican media covering El Narco has not all been rosy. Some journalists take bribes from cartels. In return, they keep gangsters' names out of their paper, put their rivals' names in, or give special attention to narco propaganda. Some of these journalists are spotted riding round in new Jeeps and building plush extensions to their homes.

But in general, the Mexican media has been a crucial, critical check on the rise of drug traffickers and shown itself in a much more positive light than other Mexican institutions such as the police or politicians.

Ioan Grillo, El Narco:
The Bloody Rise of Mexican Drug Cartels.
London, UK: Bloomsbury Press, 2011, p. 74.

According to Amnesty International the drug war creates a climate of distrust, with rumors circulating on social media as people try to protect themselves, because there is no reliable information available.

The Cartels' Response to Social Networks

The Mexican cartels have people who are experts in communications. They monitor Internet sites, blogs, phone calls and the social networks on a daily basis.

Also, with so many government officials on the take, the cartels should have access to military-level tracking technology.

According to the *Long War Journal*, given the economic resources of Los Zetas and the other cartels, a future countermove may be that of hiring additional cyber mercenaries to reinforce their defensive and offensive information operations capabilities.

The Drug Enforcement [Administration]—DEA—labels the Zetas as the most violent drug cartel operating in Mexico. In the past the Zetas have kidnapped, tortured and killed several journalists and online activists who were trying to expose the cartel's activities.

Los Zetas are deploying their own teams of computer experts to track those individuals involved in the online anti-cartel campaign, which indicates that the criminal group is taking the social media campaign against them very seriously.

After silencing local news media in many areas, they started going after their critics in social media.

While some experts believe the cartels have increased their cyber-crime capabilities, it's still unclear whether they have the expertise to track down a user on Twitter or on Facebook.

However, a Mexican cartel with hundreds of millions of dollars, certainly has the capacity to hire security experts in Mexico or former hackers.

The bottom line is: As Mexican drug war bloggers grow more sophisticated, the drug cartels are working to keep pace.

In Mexico, bloggers were tortured and beheaded. Its message was simple: Stop talking about the drug cartels on the Internet—or anywhere else.

Targeting Internet Reporters

In September 2011, two incidents occurred that represented the initial cartel counteroffensive against the civilian social networks in Mexico. The first incident happened on the 13th, linked to Los Zetas.

The mutilated bodies of two young bloggers were found hanging from a bridge, beheaded and disemboweled, with notes placed near them threatening social media users, in the Mexican border town of Nuevo Laredo.

According to CNN, the two were killed for messages they had posted on well-known Internet sites that collect reports of drug violence.

A sign was found nearby that read in Spanish, "This will happen to all the internet snitches". It then listed several websites set up to help fight drug crimes in Mexico. Police investigators claim the victims were not journalists but people from the local community, who used social media to denounce crimes.

The gruesome display appeared to mark a move by drug cartels, which have murdered journalists for their reporting, to apply the same pressure to any Mexicans who share information online.

According to CNN, the two were killed for messages they had posted on well-known Internet sites that collect reports of drug violence in areas of the country where professional journalists are no longer able to safely do their jobs.

On the 24th of September, Maria Elizabeth Macías [Castro], a 39-year-old reporter in the North Mexican border town of Nuevo Laredo, who used a community chat room to post information about crime in her city and urged fellow citizens to do the same, was found murdered on the street, next to a computer keyboard and a sign saying "OK Nuevo Laredo en

Vivo and social networks, I am Laredo Girl and I am here because of my reports and yours". Her death is also attributed to Los Zetas.

Macías did not make any effort to hide her identity because of her job in the news business, but the majority of Mexico-based drug war bloggers and tweeters hide their identities.

There were suspicions that Los Zetas were able to piece together information that led from Macías' online handle to her real identity.

On November 10 another blogger who posted under the name "Rascatripas" was found beheaded in Nuevo Laredo. Next to him there was a note that read: "This happened to me for not understanding that I shouldn't report on the social networks".

It was the fourth blogger since September reportedly killed by the Zetas. The victim helped moderate on the site *Nuevo Laredo En Vivo*.

The deaths have sent a wave of fear across social networks.

A Chilling Effect

Although cartels have successfully pressured traditional media into being quiet, they clearly feel threatened by the decentralized morphology of the web in the sense that it may be harder for them to control it.

However, the messages left with the beheaded bodies are having an impact; many bloggers have shut down their sites and many Twitter users in Mexico have been silenced.

Politicians, law enforcement, journalists and now social media users all are under attack for covering incidents involving Mexico's drug cartels.

After the incidents, the site *Frontera al Rojo Vivo* removed all of its contributors' information and archives, which makes us all think about how effective the intimidation tactics of the cartels can be.

As stated by that site: "From now on, we will only publish specific facts and information about border communities and not personal attacks".

The editors of the blog *Borderland Beat,* which has a reputation as one of the most reliable sources of information on Mexico's drug violence, say that they don't know the identity of some of the site's major contributors. Posts are often passed through intermediaries to protect secrecy.

Editors of *Blog del Narco* say they've survived by not taking sides in the drug wars.

The deaths have sent a wave of fear across social networks in Mexico. In fact, many news organizations no longer cover the violence related to the drug cartels.

Also, there is no point in denouncing something on the Internet if the authorities aren't going to do anything about it; people only expose themselves to more danger.

The last voice calling out for law and order in Mexico is in great risk of being silenced as well. Fear and lawlessness have spread from society to cyberspace.

In India, Cybercrime Is Becoming Increasingly Organized and Professional

Priyanka Joshi

Priyanka Joshi is an assistant editor at the Business Standard. *In the following viewpoint, she reports that the cybercrime economy is rapidly maturing in India. A black market is thriving, she says, in which professional criminals trade digital information, such as credit card numbers. Joshi says that the growing Indian economy is especially attractive to hackers, who engage not only in financial fraud but also in intellectual property theft and theft of defense or security secrets.*

As you read, consider the following questions:

1. Half of all data thefts are made from what kinds of locations, according to Joshi?
2. What does the ethical hacker Joshi quotes say is the main concern for illegal data sellers today in India?
3. What two approaches does Joshi say hackers use?

From compromised machines to mass e-mail lists for spamming, electronically transferring funds out of bank accounts to phishing attacks [designed to get personal information]—India's 100 million Internet users have become prime targets for hackers across the globe.

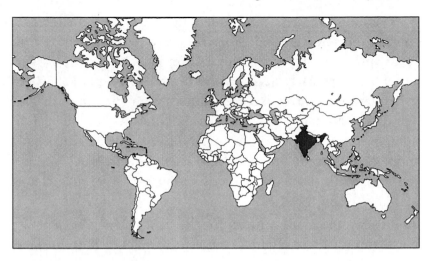

The Cybercrime Economy

A report, titled "Global Risks for 2012," shows cyber attacks on governments and businesses are considered to be one of the top five risks in the world. Be it cybercrime, cyber espionage or cyber warfare—they are on a steady rise. The reason: highly lucrative payout hackers get from stealing data. "There are high profit margins and low detection rates by law enforcement agencies. Further, half of the data thefts (on both individual PCs [personal computers] and enterprise PCs) are executed from remote or stolen server locations, which only makes prosecution difficult," points an ethical hacker employed with a large Indian IT [information technology] outsourcing company.

E-mails, personal data and financial data are the most sought after "goods" in the black market, says Pankaj Jain, director, [of the cybersecurity firm] ESET India. "The e-fraud business that has been traditionally flourishing in India is credit card cloning. The cloning itself is mostly performed by Nigerians living in India, though the card data they get are usually from Russian and former Soviet Union hackers on underground forums," he says.

Even as enterprises and individuals struggle with Internet threats, the underground cybercrime economy has moved on to organised entrepreneurship. An ethical hacker from New Delhi who regularly accesses the digital black market where cybercriminals advertise and trade stolen information and services shared how the advertisements are done. "Search, compare, and if you find a better offer we will return your money . . . ," reads an ad selling user data in black market journals. With the economic crisis looming large, such claims and ads are on the rise.

"Today, the main concern for the data sellers is to generate trust among their clients," the ethical hacker tells *Business Standard*. He added that data sellers have started offering free "trial" access to stolen bank or credit card details as well as money-back guarantees and free exchanges. "Since there is a great deal of competition in the cyber black market, the rule of supply and demand ensures that prices are competitive, with operators even offering bulk discounts to high-volume buyers," says a security consultant at a leading pharmaceutical R&D [research and development] unit in Bangalore.

Preying on Enterprise Data

The booming Indian economy, coupled with the growing buying power of individuals, is attractive to hackers. "Many industries like BPO [business process outsourcing], software, automobiles, pharmaceuticals among others are doing business across the globe from India. This certainly brings India on the wish list of hackers for data breaches and monetary gains," says Amit Nath, country manager (India & SAARC [South Asian Association for Regional Cooperation]), Trend Micro.

Hackers mostly use chance or targeted approach. "Chance approach is used when volume matters, i.e., for stealing credit card, bank account and e-mail account information. Such attacks usually consist of sending malware [software that damages or takes over a computer] or Trojans [a type of malware that masquerades as a legitimate file] through mass e-mails, social network scams and infected links," says Jain of ESET.

Government and defence data, too, are always in demand, especially by hackers in China and Pakistan.

Targeted approach is used when the criminal has a certain intent or victim in mind and the attack is tailored to make use of certain security flaws in the system. These attacks are usually used to target organisations, government or celebrities. A compromised PC could be used by a hacker in his network for attacking other computers, and also for studying the web-browsing pattern or interaction of the user on the Internet.

Today, teams of ethical hackers or security consultants work with most leading corporate and R&D outfits, tinkering with corporate IT networks to ensure the data exchanged between employees is not mishandled or, worse, stolen by rival companies.

Threats are not always limited to financial fraud alone, says Atul Khatavkar, VP (IT Governance Risk Compliance), AGC Networks. He says, "There could be cases of intellectual property theft, too. For example, the vice-president of an e-learning firm—sacked from the company later—was accused of stealing the source code of the company's future product. He subsequently used the product for his new venture, and the e-learning firm had to book nearly Rs 47 crore [that is, 470 million rupees, or over 9 million dollars] in losses due to the theft." Government and defence data, too, are always in demand, especially by hackers in China and Pakistan, lists ESET.

Not wishing to be left behind, many enterprises are leveraging on social media tools. In a report, ISACA [a nonprofit information systems association] advises that enterprises must consider the risks of employee access to social media sites while on the corporate network.

Eastern European Organized Cybercrime Rings Prey on Victims Worldwide

Brian Krebs

Brian Krebs is an American journalist and the author of the daily cybercrime and security blog Krebs on Security. *In the following viewpoint, he reports on rising numbers of data breaches in the United States that have resulted in hundreds of millions of compromised consumer records. He says that many of these security breaches are orchestrated by organized crime rings in Eastern Europe and Russia. Krebs says that where earlier hackers would simply seek out companies with weaknesses, these new organized cybercrime rings are targeting specific companies and then figuring out how to exploit them. He concludes that breaches will continue, though companies are often reluctant to disclose them.*

As you read, consider the following questions:

1. Give one example of a group that Krebs discusses to show the growing reach of organized criminal gangs in cybercrime.

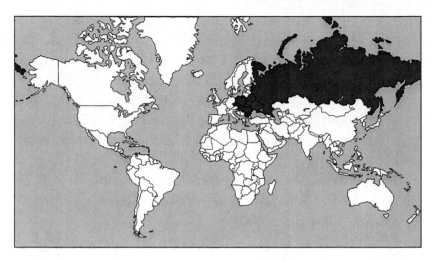

2. What is TSYS, and what data breach involving it does Krebs describe?

3. According to Krebs, what is a "sniffer" program?

A string of data breaches orchestrated principally by a handful of organized cyber-crime gangs translated into the loss of hundreds of millions of consumer records last year [2008], security experts say.

Hundreds of Millions of Records Lost

The size and scope of the breaches, some of which have previously not been disclosed, illustrate the extent that organized cyber thieves are methodically targeting computer systems connected to the global financial network.

Forensics investigators at Verizon Business, a firm hired by major companies to investigate breaches, responded to roughly 100 confirmed data breaches last year involving roughly 285 million consumer records. That staggering number—nearly one breached record for every American—exceeds the combined total breached from break-ins the company investigated from 2004 to 2007.

In all, breaches at financial institutions were responsible for 93 percent of all such records compromised last year, Verizon reported. Unlike attacks studied between 2004 and 2007—which were characterized by hackers seeking out companies that used computer software and hardware that harbored known security flaws—more than 90 percent of the records compromised in the breaches Verizon investigated in 2008 came from targeted attacks where the hackers carefully picked their targets first and then figured out a way to exploit them later.

Bryan Sartin, director of investigative response at Verizon Business, said criminals in Eastern Europe played a major role in breaches throughout 2008.

"The sophistication of these attacks has gone up, the bravado has gone up, and our commitment is steadfast."

An Eastern European Gang

"About 50 percent of the confirmed breach cases we investigated shared perpetrators," Sartin said. "Organized crime is playing a much larger part of the caseload we're seeing. We've seen that both [the FBI (Federal Bureau of Investigation)] and the Secret Service have initiatives under way to go back through their cyber crime case histories over the past several years, to start tying together all of the common characteristics of the attacks to individuals, to really try and get a firm handle on the individuals responsible for these attacks."

For example, a single organized criminal group based in Eastern Europe is believed to have hacked websites and databases belonging to hundreds of banks, payment processors, prepaid card vendors and retailers over the last year. Most of the activity from this group occurred in the first five months of 2008. But some of that activity persisted throughout the year at specific targets, according to experts who helped law enforcement officials respond to the attacks, but asked not to be identified because they are not authorized to speak on the record.

Shawn Henry, assistant director of the FBI's cyber division, said the bureau is making real progress in working with foreign law enforcement to track down the major sources of cyber crime.

"The sophistication of these attacks has gone up, the bravado has gone up, and our commitment is steadfast," Henry said. "We're working very closely with foreign law enforcement and with some of the victims, and we certainly recognize how significant these threats are coming from all over Eastern Europe."

One hacking group, which security experts say is based in Russia, attacked and infiltrated more than 300 companies—mainly financial institutions—in the United States and elsewhere, using a sophisticated web-based exploitation service that the hackers accessed remotely. In an 18-page alert published to retail and banking partners in November, Visa described this hacker service in intricate detail, listing the names of the websites and malicious software used in the attack, as well as the Internet addresses of dozens of sites that were used to off-load stolen data.

The thieves extracted money from the system by distributing the cards to dozens of so-called "money mules," who used them to withdraw millions in cash from ATMs in cities across the country.

"This information was recently used by several entities to discover security breaches that were otherwise undetected," Visa wrote.

The *Washington Post* obtained a partial list of the companies targeted by the Russian hacking group from a security researcher, which was left behind on one of the web servers the attackers used. More than a dozen companies on that list ac-

knowledged first learning about intrusions after being contacted by law enforcement agencies tracking the activities of
the cyber gang.

RBS WorldPay and Others Were Hit

This group's most high-profile and lucrative haul last year
came from Atlanta-based payment processor and payroll card
giant RBS WorldPay. In that attack, which the company disclosed on Dec. 23, 2008, the hackers siphoned nearly $10 mil-
lion from the U.S. banking system by artificially inflating the
balances on prepaid credit or cash cards. The thieves extracted
money from the system by distributing the cards to dozens of
so-called "money mules," who used them to withdraw millions
in cash from ATMs in cities across the country in a coordinated heist that took less than 24 hours.

The same hacking group also was responsible for a breach
last year at Okemo Mountain ski resort in Ludlow, Vermont.
In that attack, which Okemo disclosed on April 1, 2008, the
criminals stole payment data encoded on more than 28,000
credit and debit cards that the company processed from skiers
during a 16-day period in early February.

A month prior to that, this hacker group broke into Om-
niAmerican Bank, based in Fort Worth, Texas. As a result,
criminals were able to fabricate debit cards and PINs [per-
sonal identification numbers], and then withdraw an undis-
closed amount of cash from ATMs in Russia and Ukraine.

Other breaches attributed to this group have not been disclosed until now. The website for Euronet Worldwide, a
Leawood, Kan., based electronic payment processor that oper-
ates a major ATM network in Europe, Asia and the Middle
East, also was included on the hacker group's hit list. Euronet
spokeswoman Shruthi Fielder confirmed that the company
learned in March 2008 that "a portion of its Indian subsystem
was attacked by a sophisticated cyber-crime group through a
Web-facing program." Data concerning 38,000 bank cards was

compromised in the breach. The company said it did not pre-viously disclose the breach until contacted by a *Washington Post* reporter because the victims resided outside of the United States and beyond the reach of domestic data breach disclo-sure laws.

The attackers weren't always able to make off with cash or bank account data after successfully breaching a financial in-stitution last year. The same group of attackers also broke into TSYS [Total System Services Inc.], currently the world's second-largest credit and debit card processor on March 8, 2008.

TSYS spokesman Cyle Mims said the break-in was quickly detected and contained by the company's security staff.

"We found out about it and corrected it within hours, and no proprietary data of any kind was taken," Mims said, adding that the FBI contacted the company several months later to inform them that TSYS systems may have been targeted.

Attackers in this group also went after First Data [Retail] ATM Services, a division of Greenwood Village, Colo., based payment processor First Data Corp., which provides technology-based ATM and POS [point-of-service] solutions to financial institutions and independent sales organizations nationwide.

A spokeswoman for First Data declined to say whether the attackers were successful in breaking in. The company would say only that no personal data was stolen.

"As with many other commercial websites, Firstdataatm .com experiences unauthorized attempts to access information contained within the site," the company said in a written statement. "Our security infrastructure has been able to detect and prevent the unauthorized access of any personal informa-tion from the site."

Experts say a different cyber-crime gang operating out of Eastern Europe was responsible for what may turn out to be last year's biggest cyber heist. Princeton, N.J., based credit card processor Heartland Payment Systems disclosed on Jan. 20 that hackers had breached its systems last summer, planting malicious software designed to capture and secretly siphon account numbers as they traversed the company's internal processing networks.

Heartland, which processes roughly 100 million credit and debit card transactions per month, hasn't disclosed how many accounts may have been compromised. Company officials declined to comment for this story, citing pending class-action litigation against Heartland by entities affected by the breach. But so far, more than 600 banks have reported cards compromised as a result of the Heartland breach, according to BankInfoSecurity.com.

"There has been a considerable spike in cyber attacks against the financial services and the online retail industry."

Coordinated Cybercrime

Steve Santorelli, director of investigations at Team Cymru, a small group of researchers who work to discover who is behind Internet crime, said the hackers behind the Heartland breach and the other break-ins mentioned in this [viewpoint] appear to have been aware of one another and unofficially divided up targets.

"There seem, on the face of anecdotal observations, to be at least two main groups behind many of the major database compromises of recent years," Santorelli said. "Both groups appear to be giving each other a wide berth not to step on each others' toes."

In Feb. 2009, the Secret Service and FBI issued a rare joint advisory through Visa's website, warning banks and retailers about the techniques the hackers were using and some of the telltale signs that hackers may have broken in.

RBS WorldPay

Although most of our battles are fought face-to-face, cyber attacks are arguably more alarming, because they subtly steal our identities and slowly drain our pockets. One of the biggest cyber heists to date happened in November 2008. A transnational crime organization withdrew over $9 million in less than 12 hours from 2,100 RBS WorldPay ATMs in 280 cities throughout the U.S., Russia, Ukraine, Estonia, Italy, Japan, and Canada. Along with the money, the hackers also made off with financial data on 1.5 million customers and the Social Security numbers of 1.1 million customers.

The RBS WorldPay bank robberies were extensive due to the speed of the transactions. These speeds are widely recorded in increments of transactions per minute, per second, and per millisecond. To better understand the speed of transactions in our digital world, more than 3.7 billion standardized financial messages were exchanged in December 2009 alone, according to the Society for Worldwide Interbank Financial Telecommunication (SWIFT)....

By the time the RBS WorldPay cyber bank robbers were halted, they had already done a significant amount of damage. The victim of a sophisticated hacker ring, RBS WorldPay could just as easily have been another multinational financial organization or perhaps the bank that handles your finances.

Jeff Papows, Glitch:
The Hidden Impact of Faulty Software.
Boston, MA: Pearson Education, 2011.

"Over the past year, there has been a considerable spike in cyber attacks against the financial services and the online retail industry," the advisory begins. It goes on to list a variety of methods online merchants can use to detect and block the most common types of attacks.

In all of the specific attacks mentioned above, the methods used and tools used by the hackers were remarkably similar: The crooks scanned hundreds of financial company websites or partner sites for known security holes. Once they had exploited those holes and had made their way to the target's internal network, the attackers would install a variety of hacking tools and begin mapping the network.

According to the FBI and Secret Service, those tools usually included "sniffer" programs designed to capture credit and debit card information flowing across the bank or processor's internal networks. In addition, the crooks also installed "beacons" that allowed the attackers to connect back to the hacked sites in the future, as well as off-load stolen data.

Verizon's Sartin, said hackers last year mostly went after entities that held large stores of debit card information and corresponding PINs, information that criminals could use to extract cash from ATMs once they had imprinted the stolen data on fabricated cards.

Unlike credit card fraud, debit card fraud often hits consumers directly in the pocketbook. "ATM fraud is a much different story, because meanwhile your cash assets are missing and the burden is now on you to prove that it wasn't you who took all the money out of the account," Sartin said.

Nicholas Percoco, vice president of SpiderLabs, the incident response department at Chicago-based security vendor Trustwave, said that the methods described by federal investigators are consistent with a large number of the successful break-ins they examined.

Percoco said a majority of the breaches at financial institutions last year showed strong signs of being the work of organized criminal gangs in Russia and Eastern Europe.

In August 2008, the Justice Department announced its largest identity theft and hacking case ever prosecuted, against 11 members of what it called "international hacking rings" allegedly responsible for the theft and sale of more than 40 million debit and credit card numbers stolen from various retailers, including TJX Companies, BJ's Wholesale Club, OfficeMax, Boston Market, Barnes & Noble, Sports Authority, Forever 21 and DSW.

Sartin said that regardless of whether the criminals behind these attacks are apprehended, the breach reports from last year will be trickling in for some time, while other breaches may never be disclosed.

"About a third of the breaches investigated by our team last year are publicly disclosed. More, especially those toward the end of the year, are likely to follow. Others will likely remain unknown to the world as they do not fall under any legal disclosure requirements," he said.

Periodical and Internet Sources Bibliography

The following articles have been selected to supplement the diverse views presented in this chapter.

John E. Dunn	"Cybercrime Dominated by Organized Gangs: Study," IT World Canada, March 29, 2012. www.itworldcanada.com.
Tom Espiner	"Detica: 80 Percent of Internet Crime Is 'Co-Ordinated,'" ZDNet.com, March 29, 2012.
David Gilbert	"How the Mafia Is Ruling the World Wide Web," *International Business Times*, March 29, 2012. www.ibtimes.co.uk.
Kelly Jackson Higgins	"Russian Cybercrime Doubled Last Year to $2.3 Billion," *Dark Reading*, May 2, 2012.
Shilpa Kannan	"India Steps Up Battle Against Rising Cyber Crime Wave," BBC News, May 7, 2012.
Dan Lohrmann	"Cyber Crime: Hackers Are Hacking Each Other Too," *Government Technology*, November 6, 2011.
Martha Mendoza	"Google Takes Aim at Mexico's Drug Cartels," Associated Press, July 18, 2012.
Jason Overdorf	"India Cybercrime: We Know Who You Are, We Know What Toppings You Ordered," GlobalPost, September 13, 2012. www.globalpost.com.
Kenneth Rapoza	"Russia's Million Dollar Hackers," *Forbes*, April 24, 2012.
Matthew J. Schwartz	"Anonymous Eyes Mexican Cartel Attack," *InformationWeek*, October 31, 2011.

GLOBAL VIEWPOINTS

CHAPTER 4

Cyber Espionage and Cyberterrorism

Worldwide, State-Supported Cyber Espionage Is a Growing Danger

Economist

The Economist *is a weekly British news and business publication. In the following viewpoint, it reports that cyber warfare and cyber espionage are becoming an increasing concern for nations such as the United States and Britain. The* Economist *says cyber-espionage attacks might be able to disable a military or to shut down a financial system or a power grid. Cyber attacks are often difficult to trace, making retaliation difficult. The* Economist *says that China, Russia, the United States, and Britain are thought to be using cyber espionage. There is also fear that terrorists might begin to use cyber espionage.*

As you read, consider the following questions:

1. What caused the explosion in June 1982 that the *Economist* discusses?

2. Why does the *Economist* say that computer technology is both a blessing and a curse for the military?

3. What are SCADA systems, and why does the *Economist* say they are in increasing danger from cyber attacks?

At the height of the Cold War, in June 1982, an American early-warning satellite detected a large blast in Siberia. A missile being fired? A nuclear test? It was, it seems, an explosion on a Soviet gas pipeline. The cause was a malfunction in the computer control system that Soviet spies had stolen from a firm in Canada. They did not know that the CIA [Central Intelligence Agency] had tampered with the software so that it would "go haywire, after a decent interval, to reset pump speeds and valve settings to produce pressures far beyond those acceptable to pipeline joints and welds," according to the memoirs of Thomas Reed, a former air force secretary. The result, he said, "was the most monumental non-nuclear explosion and fire ever seen from space."

Logic Bombs

This was one of the earliest demonstrations of the power of a "logic bomb". Three decades later, with more and more vital computer systems linked up to the Internet, could enemies use logic bombs to, say, turn off the electricity from the other side of the world? Could terrorists or hackers cause financial chaos by tampering with Wall Street's computerised trading systems? And given that computer chips and software are produced globally, could a foreign power infect high-tech military equipment with computer bugs? "It scares me to death," says one senior military source. "The destructive potential is so great."

After land, sea, air and space, warfare has entered the fifth domain: cyberspace. President Barack Obama has declared America's digital infrastructure to be a "strategic national asset" and appointed Howard Schmidt, the former head of security at Microsoft, as his cybersecurity tsar. In May [2010] the Pentagon set up its new Cyber Command (Cybercom) headed by General Keith Alexander, director of the National Security Agency (NSA). His mandate is to conduct "full-spectrum" operations—to defend American military networks and attack other countries' systems. Precisely how, and by what rules, is secret.

Britain, too, has set up a cybersecurity policy outfit, and an "operations centre" based in GCHQ [Government Communications Headquarters], the British equivalent of the NSA. China talks of "winning informationised wars by the mid-21st century". Many other countries are organising for cyber war, among them Russia, Israel and North Korea. Iran boasts of having the world's second-largest cyber army.

What will cyber war look like? In a new book Richard Clarke, a former White House staffer in charge of counterterrorism and cybersecurity, envisages a catastrophic breakdown within 15 minutes. Computer bugs bring down military e-mail systems; oil refineries and pipelines explode; air-traffic-control systems collapse; freight and metro trains derail; financial data are scrambled; the electrical grid goes down in the eastern United States; orbiting satellites spin out of control. Society soon breaks down as food becomes scarce and money runs out. Worst of all, the identity of the attacker may remain a mystery.

The Internet was designed for convenience and reliability, not security.

In the view of Mike McConnell, a former spy chief, the effects of full-blown cyber war are much like nuclear attack. Cyber war has already started, he says, "and we are losing it." Not so, retorts Mr Schmidt. There is no cyber war. Bruce Schneier, an IT [information technology] industry security guru, accuses securocrats like Mr Clarke of scaremongering. Cyberspace will certainly be part of any future war, he says, but an apocalyptic attack on America is both difficult to achieve technically ("movie-script stuff") and implausible except in the context of a real war, in which case the perpetrator is likely to be obvious.

Computer Strength, Computer Vulnerability

For the top brass, computer technology is both a blessing and a curse. Bombs are guided by GPS [global positioning system] satellites; drones are piloted remotely from across the world; fighter planes and warships are now huge data-processing centres; even the ordinary foot soldier is being wired up. Yet growing connectivity over an insecure Internet multiplies the avenues for e-attack; and growing dependence on computers increases the harm they can cause.

By breaking up data and sending it over multiple routes, the Internet can survive the loss of large parts of the network. Yet some of the global digital infrastructure is more fragile. More than nine-tenths of Internet traffic travels through undersea fibre-optic cables, and these are dangerously bunched up in a few choke points, for instance around New York, the Red Sea or the Luzon Strait in the Philippines. Internet traffic is directed by just 13 clusters of potentially vulnerable domain-name servers. Other dangers are coming: weakly governed swathes of Africa are being connected up to fibre-optic cables, potentially creating new havens for cybercriminals. And the spread of mobile Internet will bring new means of attack.

The Internet was designed for convenience and reliability, not security. Yet in wiring together the globe, it has merged the garden and the wilderness. No passport is required in cyberspace. And although police are constrained by national borders, criminals roam freely. Enemy states are no longer on the other side of the ocean, but just behind the firewall. The ill-intentioned can mask their identity and location, impersonate others and con their way into the buildings that hold the digitised wealth of the electronic age: money, personal data and intellectual property.

$1 Trillion in Cybercrime

Mr Obama has quoted a figure of $1 trillion lost last year [2009] to cybercrime—a bigger underworld than the drugs trade, though such figures are disputed. Banks and other companies do not like to admit how much data they lose. In 2008 alone Verizon, a telecoms company, recorded the loss of 285m personal-data records, including credit-card and bank-account details, in investigations conducted for clients.

About nine-tenths of the 140 billion e-mails sent daily are spam; of these about 16% contain moneymaking scams, including "phishing" attacks that seek to dupe recipients into giving out passwords or bank details, according to Symantec, a security software vendor. The amount of information now available online about individuals makes it ever easier to attack a computer by crafting a personalised e-mail that is more likely to be trusted and opened. This is known as "spear phishing".

"Given enough time, motivation and funding, a determined adversary will always—always—be able to penetrate a targeted system."

The ostentatious hackers and virus writers who once wrecked computers for fun are all but gone, replaced by criminal gangs seeking to harvest data. "Hacking used to be about making noise. Now it's about staying silent," says Greg Day of McAfee, a vendor of IT security products. Hackers have become wholesale providers of malware—viruses, worms and Trojans that infect computers—for others to use. Websites are now the favoured means of spreading malware, partly because the unwary are directed to them through spam or links posted on social networking sites. And poorly designed websites often provide a window into valuable databases.

Malware is exploding. It is typically used to steal passwords and other data, or to open a "back door" to a computer so that it can be taken over by outsiders. Such "zombie" machines can be linked up to thousands, if not millions, of others around the world to create a "botnet". Estimates for the number of infected machines range up to 100m. Botnets are used to send spam, spread malware or launch distributed denial-of-service (DDoS) attacks, which seek to bring down a targeted computer by overloading it with countless bogus requests.

The Spy Who Spammed Me

Criminals usually look for easy prey. But states can combine the criminal hackers' tricks, such as spear phishing, with the intelligence apparatus to reconnoitre [survey] a target, the computing power to break codes and passwords, and the patience to probe a system until it finds a weakness—usually a fallible human being. Steven Chabinsky, a senior FBI [Federal Bureau of Investigation] official responsible for cybersecurity, recently said that "given enough time, motivation and funding, a determined adversary will always—always—be able to penetrate a targeted system."

Traditional human spies risk arrest or execution by trying to smuggle out copies of documents. But those in the cyber world face no such risks. "A spy might once have been able to take out a few books' worth of material," says one senior American military source. "Now they take the whole library. And if you restock the shelves, they will steal it again."

China, in particular, is accused of wholesale espionage, attacking the computers of major Western defence contractors and reputedly taking classified details of the F-35 fighter, the

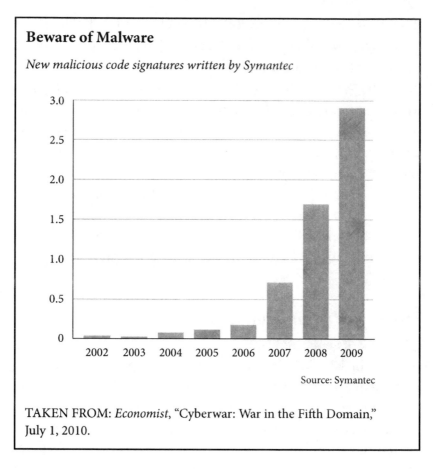

Beware of Malware

New malicious code signatures written by Symantec

Source: Symantec

TAKEN FROM: *Economist*, "Cyberwar: War in the Fifth Domain," July 1, 2010.

mainstay of future American air power. At the end of 2009 it appears to have targeted Google and more than a score of other IT companies. Experts at a cyber test-range built in Maryland by Lockheed Martin, a defence contractor (which denies losing the F-35 data), say "advanced persistent threats" are hard to fend off amid the countless minor probing of its networks. Sometimes attackers try to slip information out slowly, hidden in ordinary Internet traffic. At other times they have tried to break in by leaving infected memory sticks in the car park, hoping somebody would plug them into the network. Even unclassified e-mails can contain a wealth of useful information about projects under development.

"Cyber espionage is the biggest intelligence disaster since the loss of the nuclear secrets [in the late 1940s]," says Jim Lewis of the Center for Strategic and International Studies, a think tank in Washington, DC. Spying probably presents the most immediate danger to the West: the loss of high-tech know-how that could erode its economic lead or, if it ever came to a shooting war, blunt its military edge.

Western spooks think China deploys the most assiduous, and most shameless, cyber spies, but Russian ones are probably more skilled and subtle. Top of the league, say the spooks, are still America's NSA and Britain's GCHQ, which may explain why Western countries have until recently been reluctant to complain too loudly about computer snooping.

The next step after penetrating networks to steal data is to disrupt or manipulate them. If military targeting information could be attacked, for example, ballistic missiles would be useless. Those who play war games speak of being able to "change the red and blue dots": make friendly (blue) forces appear to be the enemy (red), and vice versa.

General Alexander says the Pentagon and NSA started cooperating on cyber warfare in late 2008 after "a serious intrusion into our classified networks". Mr Lewis says this refers to the penetration of Central Command, which oversees the wars in Iraq and Afghanistan, through an infected thumb drive. It took a week to winkle out the intruder. Nobody knows what, if any, damage was caused. But the thought of an enemy lurking in battle-fighting systems alarms the top brass.

That said, an attacker might prefer to go after unclassified military logistics supply systems, or even the civilian infrastructure. A loss of confidence in financial data and electronic transfers could cause economic upheaval. An even bigger worry is an attack on the power grid. Power companies tend not to keep many spares of expensive generator parts, which can take months to replace. Emergency diesel generators cannot make up for the loss of the grid, and cannot operate indefinitely. Without electricity and other critical services, communications systems and cash dispensers cease to work. A loss of power lasting just a few days, reckon some, starts to cause a cascade of economic damage.

Experts disagree about the vulnerability of systems that run industrial plants, known as supervisory control and data acquisition (SCADA). But more and more of these are being connected to the Internet, raising the risk of remote attack. "Smart grids", which relay information about energy use to the utilities, are promoted as ways of reducing energy waste. But they also increase security worries about both crime (e.g., allowing bills to be falsified) and exposing SCADA networks to attack.

General Alexander has spoken of "hints that some penetrations are targeting systems for remote sabotage". But precisely what is happening is unclear: Are outsiders probing SCADA systems only for reconnaissance, or to open "back doors" for future use? One senior American military source said that if any country were found to be planting logic bombs on the grid, it would provoke the equivalent of the Cuban missile crisis.

Many assume that both these attacks were instigated by the Kremlin.

Estonia, Georgia and Web War 1

Important thinking about the tactical and legal concepts of cyber warfare is taking place in a former Soviet barracks in Estonia, now home to NATO's [North Atlantic Treaty Organization's] "centre of excellence" for cyber defence. It was established in response to what has become known as "Web War 1", a concerted denial-of-service attack on Estonian government, media and bank web servers that was precipitated by the decision to move a Soviet-era war memorial in central

Tallinn in 2007. This was more a cyber riot than a war, but it forced Estonia more or less to cut itself off from the Internet.

Similar attacks during Russia's war with Georgia the next year looked more ominous, because they seemed to be co-ordinated with the advance of Russian military columns. Government and media websites went down and telephone lines were jammed, crippling Georgia's ability to present its case abroad. President Mikheil Saakashvili's website had to be moved to an American server better able to fight off the attack. Estonian experts were dispatched to Georgia to help out.

Many assume that both these attacks were instigated by the Kremlin [that is, the Russian government]. But investigations traced them only to Russian "hacktivists" and criminal botnets; many of the attacking computers were in Western countries. There are wider issues: Did the cyber attack on Estonia, a member of NATO, count as an armed attack, and should the alliance have defended it? And did Estonia's assistance to Georgia, which is not in NATO, risk drawing Estonia into the war, and NATO along with it?

Such questions permeate discussions of NATO's new "strategic concept", to be adopted later this year. A panel of experts headed by Madeleine Albright, a former American secretary of state, reported in May that cyber attacks are among the three most likely threats to the alliance. The next significant attack, it said, "may well come down a fibre-optic cable" and may be serious enough to merit a response under the mutual-defence provisions of Article 5 [of the NATO treaty].

During his confirmation hearing, senators sent General Alexander several questions. Would he have "significant" offensive cyber weapons? Might these encourage others to follow suit? How sure would he need to be about the identity of an attacker to "fire back"? Answers to these were restricted to a classified supplement. In public the general said that the president would be the judge of what constituted cyber war; if America responded with force in cyberspace it would be in keeping with the rules of war and the "principles of military necessity, discrimination, and proportionality".

General Alexander's seven-month confirmation process is a sign of the qualms senators felt at the merging of military and espionage functions, the militarisation of cyberspace and the fear that it may undermine Americans' right to privacy. Cyber Command will protect only the military ".mil" domain. The government domain, ".gov", and the corporate infrastructure, ".com", will be the responsibility respectively of the Department of Homeland Security and private companies, with support from Cybercom.

Cyber weapons are most effective in the hands of big states. But because they are cheap, they may be most useful to the comparatively weak.

One senior military official says General Alexander's priority will be to improve the defences of military networks. Another bigwig casts some doubt on cyber offence. "It's hard to do it at a specific time," he says. "If a cyber attack is used as a military weapon, you want a predictable time and effect. If you are using it for espionage it does not matter; you can wait." He implies that cyber weapons would be used mainly as an adjunct to conventional operations in a narrow theatre.

The Chinese may be thinking the same way. A report on China's cyber-warfare doctrine, written for the congressionally mandated US-China Economic and Security Review Commission, envisages China using cyber weapons not to defeat America, but to disrupt and slow down its forces long enough for China to seize Taiwan without having to fight a shooting war.

Apocalypse or Asymmetry?

Deterrence in cyber warfare is more uncertain than, say, in nuclear strategy: There is no mutually assured destruction, the dividing line between criminality and war is blurred and identifying attacking computers, let alone the fingers on the keyboards, is difficult. Retaliation need not be confined to cyberspace; the one system that is certainly not linked to the public Internet is America's nuclear firing chain. Still, the more likely use of cyber weapons is probably not to bring about electronic apocalypse, but as tools of limited warfare.

Cyber weapons are most effective in the hands of big states. But because they are cheap, they may be most useful to the comparatively weak. They may well suit terrorists. Fortunately, perhaps, the likes of [terrorist group] al-Qaeda have mostly used the Internet for propaganda and communication. It may be that jihadists lack the ability to, say, induce a refinery to blow itself up. Or it may be that they prefer the gory theatre of suicide bombings to the anonymity of computer sabotage—for now.

The United States and Israel Launched a Cyber Attack upon Iran

Joby Warrick

Joby Warrick is a journalist at the Washington Post *and the author of* The Triple Agent: The al-Qaeda Mole Who Infiltrated the CIA. *In the following viewpoint, he reports that the United States and Israel worked together to create a cyber attack that could disrupt the Iranian nuclear program. Though Iranians say that the program is peaceful, the United States and Israel believe that Iran is trying to develop a nuclear bomb. Warrick says that the cyber weapon, called Stuxnet, was meant to cause mishaps at nuclear plants that would be undetectable and blamed on Iranian scientists. Though the attack was successful, Iran insists its nuclear program will continue.*

As you read, consider the following questions:

1. When was Stuxnet developed, according to Warrick?

2. Warrick says that Iran referred obliquely to the cyber attack? What did Iranian officials say?

3. According to Warrick, when did Stuxnet start to show effects, and what were those effects?

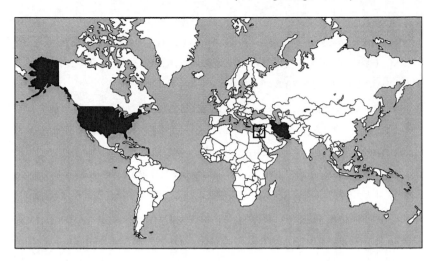

A damaging cyberattack against Iran's nuclear program was the work of U.S. and Israeli experts and proceeded under the secret orders of President Barack Obama, who was eager to slow that nation's apparent progress toward building an atomic bomb without launching a traditional military attack, current and former U.S. officials say.

Stuxnet

The origins of the cyber weapon, which outside analysts dubbed Stuxnet after it was inadvertently discovered in 2010, have long been debated, with most experts concluding that the United States and Israel probably collaborated on the effort. The current and former U.S. officials confirmed that long-standing suspicion Friday [in June 2012], after a *New York Times* report on the program.

The officials, speaking on condition of anonymity to describe the classified effort code-named Olympic Games, said it was first developed during the George W. Bush administration and was geared toward damaging Iran's nuclear capability gradually while sowing confusion among Iranian scientists about the cause of mishaps at a nuclear plant.

The use of the cyber weapon, malware designed to infiltrate and damage systems run by computers, was supposed to make the Iranians think their engineers were incapable of running an enrichment facility.

Overall, the attack destroyed nearly 1,000 of Iran's 6,000 centrifuges, fast-spinning machines that enrich uranium, an essential step toward building an atomic bomb.

"The idea was to string it out as long as possible," one participant in the operation said. "If you had wholesale destruction right away, then they generally can figure out what happened, and it doesn't look like incompetence."

Even after software-security companies discovered Stuxnet loose on the Internet in 2010, Obama secretly ordered the operation continued and authorized the use of several variations of the computer virus.

Overall, the attack destroyed nearly 1,000 of Iran's 6,000 centrifuges, fast-spinning machines that enrich uranium, an essential step toward building an atomic bomb. The National Security Agency [NSA] developed the cyber weapon with help of Israel.

Several senior Iranian officials on Friday referred obliquely to the cyberattack in reaffirming Iran's intention to expand its nuclear program.

"Despite all plots and mischievous behavior of the Western countries . . . Iran did not withdraw one iota from its rights," Kazem Seddiqi, a senior Iranian cleric, said during services at a Tehran University mosque, according to news reports from Iran.

Iran previously has blamed U.S. and Israeli officials and has said its nuclear program is solely for peaceful purposes, such as generating electricity.

White House officials declined to comment on the new details about Stuxnet, and an administration spokesman denied that the material had been leaked for political advantage.

"This officially signals the beginning of the cyber arms race in practice and not in theory."

"It's our view, as it is the view of everybody who handles classified information, that information is classified for a reason: that it is kept secret," deputy press secretary Josh Earnest told reporters. "It is intended not to be publicized, because publicizing it would pose a threat to our national security."

The revelations come at a particularly sensitive time, as the United States and five other world powers are engaged in talks with Iran on proposed cuts to its nuclear program. Iran has refused to agree to concessions on what it says is its rightful pursuit of peaceful nuclear energy. The next round of negotiations is scheduled for this month in Moscow.

Cyber War

"Effectively, the United States has gone to war with Iran and has chosen to do so in this manner because the effects can justify this means," said Rafal Rohozinski, a cyber expert and principal of the SecDev Group, referring to the slowing of Iran's nuclear program.

"This officially signals the beginning of the cyber arms race in practice and not in theory," Rohozinski said.

In 2006, senior Bush administration officials developed the idea of using a computer worm, with Israeli assistance, to damage Iranian centrifuges at its uranium-enrichment plant in Natanz. The concept originated with Gen. James Cartwright, who was then head of the U.S. Strategic Command, which handles nuclear deterrence, and had a reputation as a cyber strategist.

Stuxnet: A New Cyber Attack

Since it was first discovered in June of 2010, Stuxnet, a highly sophisticated malicious software program, or malware, has created a huge stir throughout the computer-security industry. Most malware is used by cyber criminals to steal proprietary data such as credit card information and business plans or to harness groups of computers together for use in a botnet [a group of computers that have been taken over by a malicious third party]. What sets Stuxnet apart and makes it a deadly new breed of malware is that Stuxnet is designed to silently sabotage infected computers. Specifically, Stuxnet targets Siemens [AG] software systems, a company that designs operating systems for large industrial facilities like nuclear power plants.

Stuxnet worms its way into a computer and looks for very specific Siemens Programmable Logic Controller (PLC) settings, a digital fingerprint that tells the malware that it has found its target, and then injects its own code into the operating system. If Stuxnet determines that the system is not its target, then it moves on, causing no damage. Once Stuxnet injects its new code into the PLC device, it causes silent failure of crucial aspects of the plant's systems, such as centrifuges or heating and cooling systems that are undetectable until the damage is already done. In other words, Stuxnet was not an indiscriminant killer, it was searching for a very specific real-world target, "a cyber weapon created to cross from the digital realm to the physical world—to destroy something."

Nat Katin-Borland, "Cyberwar: A Real and Growing Threat,"
Cyberspaces and Global Affairs. *Eds. Sean S. Costigan and Jake Perry.*
Burlington, VT: Ashgate Publishing, 2012, pp. 13–14.

"Cartwright's role was describing the art of the possible, having a view or vision," said a former senior official familiar with the program. But "the heavy lifting" was done by NSA director Keith Alexander, who had "the technical know-how and carried out the actual activity," the former official said.

Olympic Games became a collaborative effort among the NSA, the CIA [Central Intelligence Agency] and Israel, current and former officials said. The CIA, under then director Michael Hayden, lent its covert operation authority to the program.

The CIA and Israelis oversaw the development of plans to gain physical access to the plant. Installing the worm in plant equipment not connected to the Internet depended on spies and unwitting accomplices who might connect an infected device to one of the systems, officials said.

The cyber weapon took months of testing and development. It began to show effects in 2008, when centrifuges began spinning at faster-than-normal speeds until sensitive components began to warp and break, participants said.

Tibetan Exiles May Be the Target of Chinese Cyber Espionage

Information Warfare Monitor

The Information Warfare Monitor (IWM) was an advanced research project based in Canada that tracked the emergence of cyberspace as a strategic domain; the project closed in 2012. In the following viewpoint, IWM reports on its research into GhostNet, a cyber-espionage network that infiltrated many strategic computers associated with the Tibetan exile community. IWM suggests that China is a likely source of GhostNet, though no certain attribution is possible. IWM concludes that nations and organizations must pay more attention to cybersecurity and suggests that in the future there will be more cyber-espionage networks such as GhostNet.

As you read, consider the following questions:

1. What are the three key findings of IWM's investigation?

2. What two examples does IWM give of instances in which Chinese hackers, not necessarily associated with the Chinese government, focused on nationalist targets?

3. What is "social engineering," and how can it be used to spread malware, according to IWM?

"Tracking *GhostNet*: Investigating a Cyber Espionage Network," Information Warfare Monitor (IWM), March 29, 2009, pp. 5–49. Copyright © 2009 by IWM. All rights reserved. Reproduced by permission.

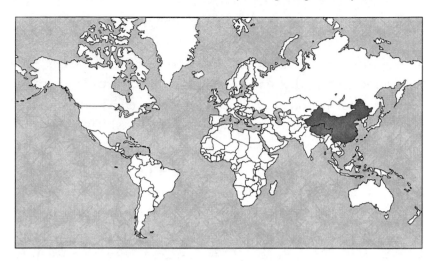

Trojan horse programmes [in which harmful code is disguised in apparently harmless programming] and other associated malware [malicious software] are often cited as vectors for conducting sophisticated computer-based espionage. Allegations of cyber espionage (computer network exploitation) are increasingly common, but there are few case studies in the unclassified realm that expose the inner workings of such networks.

China, Tibet, and Cyber Espionage

This study reveals the existence and operational reach of a malware-based cyber espionage network that we call *GhostNet*.

Between June 2008 and March 2009, the Information Warfare Monitor conducted an extensive and exhaustive two-phase investigation focused on allegations of Chinese cyber espionage against the Tibetan community.[1]

We conducted field-based investigations in India, Europe and North America. In India we worked directly with affected Tibetan organizations, including the private office of the Dalai Lama [the spiritual leader of Tibet], the Tibetan Government-

---

1. Tibet is controlled by China. Many Tibetans have fled; therefore, there is an important Tibetan exile community.

in-Exile, and several Tibetan NGOs [nongovernmental organizations]. In Europe and North America we worked with Tibetan missions in London, Brussels, and New York. The fieldwork generated extensive data that allowed us to examine Tibetan information security practices as well as capture *real-time* evidence of malware that had penetrated Tibetan computer systems.

During the second phase of our investigation, the data was analyzed, and led to the discovery of insecure, web-based interfaces to four control servers. These interfaces allow attacker(s) to send instructions to, and receive data from, compromised computers. Our research team successfully scouted these servers, revealing a wide-ranging network of compromised computers. This extensive network consists of at least 1,295 infected computers in 103 countries.

Significantly, close to 30% of the infected computers can be considered high-value and include the ministries of foreign affairs of Iran, Bangladesh, Latvia, Indonesia, Philippines, Brunei, Barbados, and Bhutan; embassies of India, South Korea, Indonesia, Romania, Cyprus, Malta, Thailand, Taiwan, Portugal, Germany, and Pakistan; the ASEAN (Association of Southeast Asian Nations) Secretariat, SAARC (South Asian Association for Regional Cooperation), and the Asian Development Bank; news organizations; and an unclassified computer located at NATO [North Atlantic Treaty Organization] headquarters.

The *GhostNet* system directs infected computers to download a Trojan known as *Gh0st RAT* that allows attackers to gain complete, *real-time* control. These instances of *Gh0st RAT* are consistently controlled from commercial Internet-access accounts located on the island of Hainan, People's Republic of China.

Our investigation reveals that *GhostNet* is capable of taking full control of infected computers, including searching and downloading specific files, and covertly operating attached devices, including microphones and web cameras.

The vector for spreading the *GhostNet* infection leverages social means. Contextually relevant e-mails are sent to specific targets with attached documents that are packed with *exploit code* and Trojan horse programmes designed to take advantage of vulnerabilities in software installed on the target's computer.

Once compromised, files located on infected computers may be mined for contact information, and used to spread malware through e-mail and document attachments that appear to come from legitimate sources, and contain legitimate documents and messages. It is therefore possible that the large percentage of high-value targets identified in our analysis of the *GhostNet* are coincidental, spread by contact between individuals who previously communicated through e-mail.

Nonetheless the existence of the *GhostNet* network is a significant fact in and of itself. At the very least, it demonstrates the ease by which computer-based malware can be used to build a robust, low-cost intelligence capability and infect a network of potentially high-value targets.

Key findings:

- Documented evidence of a cyber espionage network— *GhostNet*—infecting at least 1,295 computers in 103 countries, of which close to 30% can be considered as high-value diplomatic, political, economic, and military targets.

- Documented evidence of *GhostNet* penetration of computer systems containing sensitive and secret information at the private offices of the Dalai Lama and other Tibetan targets.

- Documentation and reverse engineering of the *modus operandi* of the *GhostNet* system—including vectors, targeting, delivery mechanisms, data retrieval, and control systems—reveals a covert, difficult-to-detect, and elaborate cyber espionage system capable of taking full control of affected systems. . . .

Alleged Chinese Operations in Cyberspace

China has been developing its cyberspace doctrine and capabilities since the late 1990s as part of its military modernization programme. The Chinese doctrine of 'active defence' which is the belief that China must be ready to respond to aggression immediately, places an emphasis on the development of cyber warfare capabilities.

The Chinese focus on cyber capabilities as part of its strategy of national asymmetric warfare involves deliberately developing capabilities that circumvent U.S. superiority in command-and-control warfare. The strategy recognizes the critical importance of the cyber domain to American military and economic power and the importance of offensive cyber operations to victory in a modern conflict with the United States. Chinese doctrine also emphasizes the contiguity between military and nonmilitary realms.

Determining those responsible for cyber attacks, commonly known as the attribution problem, *is a major challenge.*

In recent years, there has been an increase in allegations that China-based hackers are responsible for high-level penetrations of computer systems in Europe, North America, and Asia. Attackers originating in China have been accused of infiltrating government computers in the United States, Britain, France, Germany, South Korea, and Taiwan. China-based hackers have been accused of data theft from foreign government computers and commercial and financial institutions. The U.S. Department of Defense reports it is continuously targeted by Chinese attackers, most notably in the series of attacks since 2003 known as 'Titan Rain,' which targeted the Department of Defense and numerous defence companies.

There are also allegations of attacks originating from China directed against nongovernmental organizations active in regions where China has a national interest. This includes organizations advocating on the conflict in the Darfur region of Sudan, Tibetan groups active in India, and the Falun Gong [a spiritual discipline whose practitioners China has vigorously persecuted]. The majority of attacks involve website defacements, denial-of-service attacks, or virus-writing campaigns. Nationalistic and patriotic cyber activity by Chinese nationals intensifies during crises, such as during Sino-American or Sino-Taiwanese[2] tensions. To date none of these attacks have been traced back to Chinese state authorities or specific individuals, although many have benefited official Chinese policy and interests.

The Attribution Problem

Determining those responsible for cyber attacks, commonly known as the *attribution problem*, is a major challenge. The Internet was never built with security as a priority. The current version of the Internet's address assignment system, IPv4 [Internet Protocol version 4], provides a wealth of loopholes and methods by which a perpetrator can mask his or her real identity and location. Online identities and servers can be cleverly hidden. Packet flows and connections can be masked and redirected through multiple servers. A clever attacker can often hijack a machine belonging to an otherwise innocent organization and use it as a base for launching attacks.

Hand in hand with the problem of attribution is the difficulty of identifying motivating factors behind a cyber attack. Many perpetrators of Internet-based attacks and exploits are individuals whose motivation can vary from a simple profit

2. Taiwan is an island near the coast of Japan with which China has tense relations.

motive through to fear of prosecution or strong emotional feelings, including religious belief and nationalism. Many cyber attacks and exploits which *seem* to benefit states may be the work of third-party actors operating under a variety of motivations. This makes it difficult to separate the motivation of the individual from the potential motives of the party on whose behalf the attacks have occurred, or a prospective client to which the perpetrator is trying to market his or her wares. In either case, the challenge of identifying perpetrators and understanding their motives gives state actors convenient *plausible deniability* and the ability to officially distance themselves from attacks.

Earlier research has traced these attacks against Tibetan groups to IP addresses registered in the People's Republic of China.

Cyber campaigns can also take on a life of their own. Even though a state might 'seed' a particular campaign through tacit encouragement or the absence of sanctions or prosecutions, these campaigns are inherently chaotic and unpredictable in scope and outcome. Phenomena such as spontaneous 'cyber rioting' can surpass the initial purposes of the cyber campaign. Low barriers to entry to this sort of activity enable anyone with a computer and Internet connection to take part in a cyber attack. For the most part, governments appear to passively benefit from online manifestations of nationalistic and patriotic fervour, although outcomes are inherently unpredictable.

In China, the authorities most likely perceive individual attackers and their online activities as convenient instruments of national power. A favourite target of Chinese hackers is Taiwanese computer systems, especially during times of Sino-Taiwanese tensions, such as elections and referendums. In April 2001, following the death of a Chinese fighter pilot after a collision with an American spy plane near the Chinese island of Hainan, Chinese hackers began a sustained campaign to target American computer networks. No link was made with elements of the Chinese government.

However, governments cannot always preserve direct control over such activities; groups can maintain their freelance and autonomous status and undertake their own cyber initiatives that may not always attain official sanction or serve state interests.

Targeting Tibet

Accusations of Chinese *cyber war* being waged against the Tibetan community have been commonplace for the past several years. The Chinese government has been accused of orchestrating and encouraging such activity as part of a wider strategy to crack down on dissident groups and subversive activity. Earlier research has traced these attacks against Tibetan groups to IP addresses registered in the People's Republic of China. The attacks used malware hidden in legitimate-looking e-mail messages, infecting unsuspecting users' computers, and exploiting the data on it by sending it to control servers.

The identity of the attackers has never been attributed in a conclusive manner to any specific group or individual. The motivation of those behind the attacks, despite conjecture, is also unproven.

In earlier studies, researchers focused on attacks specifically targeting the Tibetan community. But a wide variety of other victims of computer penetrations have reported infections similar to those used against Tibetan organizations, following a similar *modus operandi* and also reporting to control servers usually located in China. These additional targets include the Falun Gong, the U.S. government, and multinational corporations. While reports of these targeted attacks have circulated, the extent to which attackers successfully exploited the affected computers is unknown.

The Geographic Location of Host Computers Infected by *GhostNet*

Total IPs: 986
Total Number of Countries: 93

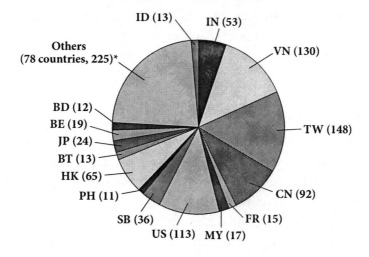

ID	Indonesia	**BD**	Bangladesh
IN	India	**BE**	Belgium
VN	Vietnam	**JP**	Japan
TW	Taiwan	**BT**	Bhutan
CN	China	**HK**	Hong Kong
FR	France	**PH**	Philippines
MY	Malaysia	**SB**	Solomon Islands
		US	United States

* This graphic illustrates the global reach of the *GhostNet*. There were 1,295 infected computers that reported to the control server. The infections were spread across 103 countries.

TAKEN FROM: "Tracking *GhostNet*: Investigating a Cyber Espionage Network," Information Warfare Monitor, March 29, 2009, p. 41.

From June 2008 to March 2009 the Information Warfare Monitor conducted an in-depth investigation of alleged cyber espionage against the Tibetan community. We chose this case study because of the unprecedented access that we were granted to Tibetan institutions through one of our researchers and persistent allegations that confidential information on secure computers was somehow being compromised. Our lead field investigator had a long history of working with the Tibetan community, and was able to work with the private office of the Dalai Lama, the Tibetan Government-in-Exile, and a number of Tibetan nongovernmental organizations. . . .

Evidence of Malware

We conducted our investigation in Dharamsala [in India, a center of the Tibetan community in exile] between July and September 2008. The initial purpose was to gather targeted malware samples from Tibetan NGOs based in the area and to brief the Tibetan Government-in-Exile (TGIE) on the basics of information security. This included raising end-user awareness about social engineering and its policy implications for the secure use of information systems.

The investigator met with the Dalai Lama's representative in Geneva, Tseten Samdup. During the meeting, Samdup inquired about the potential threat to computer security at the Office of His Holiness the Dalai Lama (OHHDL) in light of the targeted malware threat. Samdup requested that the investigator perform a preliminary security review of OHHDL systems, including Dalailama.com and the office computer network. A five-day mission was scheduled in early September. Malware was discovered on computers located in the OHHDL.

Following the discovery of malware in the OHHDL, our investigator shifted focus to the campus network of the Tibetan Government-in-Exile. We approached Thubten Samphel, a senior civil servant in the Department of Information and International Relations, and sought permission to run Wireshark on several key computer systems, and to access the firewall logs at the Tibetan Computing Resource Centre. This access was readily granted.

Additional testing was carried out at a Tibetan NGO. This was done at the suggestion of Phuntsok Dorjee, the director of a local NGO, TibTec [Tibetan Technology Center]. Dorjee suggested that we conduct testing and monitoring at the offices of Drewla. As was the case at other sites the investigator conducted a series of interviews with the NGO staff.

In September 2002, Tibetan groups reported that they were targeted with malware originating from servers in mainland China. They claimed that this was a coordinated attempt to disrupt their operations and *spy* on their computer networks. Similar attacks have occurred since then against a range of Tibetan non-state actors, including exile groups, human rights organizations, trade unions and labour organizers, writers, scholars, and intellectuals.

In 2005, a member of our investigating team convened a working group that coordinated the collection and archiving of the malware, including the payloads and associated examples of social engineering employed. Since early 2008, we have analysed every sample available to us, and identified control servers for at least fifty incidents.

During an analysis of attacks which occurred during the 2008 Beijing Olympics, we discovered the location of a control server that was later identified as part of the network which infected a computer in the private office of the Dalai Lama.

We were able to gain access to the command *interface* of this control server and identify the infected computers which reported back to this server. While we are unable to prove exactly how the computer in the Dalai Lama's office became infected, this case demonstrates one of the attack vectors used by the attacker(s) behind the network of infected computers we later uncovered.

The following steps illustrate the attack vector using the malicious document we collected, which was configured to connect to a control server to which we later acquired access.

An e-mail message arrives in the target's in-box carrying the malware in an attachment or web link. The attacker's objective is to get the target to open the attachment or malicious link so that the malicious code can execute. In this case, the attacker(s) sent a carefully crafted e-mail message which was configured to appear as if it was sent from campaigns @freetibet.org with an attached infected Word document named "Translation of Freedom Movement ID Book for Tibetans in Exile.doc" to entice the recipient to open the file.

These Trojans generally allow for near-unrestricted access to the infected system.

Over time, it has been observed that the carrier e-mails have become more sophisticated in their targeting and content in order to trick their recipients into believing that they are receiving legitimate messages. This is also known as "social engineering." It is common to see legitimate documents recycled for such attacks or the attacker injecting their message into an ongoing group conversation. There are also cases where it appears that content stolen from previously infected machines was recycled to enhance the appearance of legitimacy.

The targeted user proceeds to open the attachment or malicious link. Once opened, the infected file or link exploits a vulnerability on the user's machine and installs the malware on the user's computer, along with a seemingly benign file. From the user's perspective, the infected document will often open normally, leaving the user unaware of the infection that just took place.

Only 11 of the 34 anti-virus programmes provided by VirusTotal recognized the malware embedded in the document. Attackers often use executable packers to obfuscate their malicious code in order to avoid detection by anti-virus software.

Researchers monitoring the use of socially engineered malware attacks against the Tibetan community have identified over eight different Trojan families in use. Control over some targeted machines is maintained using the Chinese *Gh0st RAT*. These Trojans generally allow for near-unrestricted access to the infected systems.

Who Is in Control?

Who is ultimately in control of the *GhostNet* system? While our analysis reveals that numerous politically sensitive and high-value computer systems were compromised, we do not know the motivation or the identity of the attacker(s) or how to accurately characterize this network of infections as a whole. We have not been able to ascertain the type of data that has been obtained by the attacker(s), apart from the basic system information and file listings of the documents located on the target computers. Without this data we are unable to deduce with any certainty what kind of data the attacker(s) were after. There are thus several possibilities for attribution.

The most obvious explanation, and certainly the one in which the circumstantial evidence tilts the strongest, would be that this set of high-profile targets has been exploited by the Chinese state for military and strategic-intelligence purposes. Indeed, as described above, many of the high-confidence, high-value targets that we identified are clearly linked to Chinese foreign and defence policy, particularly in South and Southeast Asia. Like radar sweeping around the southern border of China, there is an arc of infected nodes from India, Bhutan, Bangladesh, and Vietnam, through Laos, Brunei, Philippines, Hong Kong, and Taiwan. Many of the high-profile targets reflect some of China's most vexing foreign and security policy issues, including Tibet and Taiwan. Moreover, the attacker's IP addresses examined here trace back in at least several instances to Hainan Island, home of the Lingshui signals intelligence facility and the Third Department of the People's Liberation Army [of China].

However, we must be cautious to rush to judgment in spite of circumstantial and other evidence, as alternative explanations are certainly possible and charges against a government of this nature are gravely serious. On the other end of the spectrum is the explanation that this is a random set of infected computers that just happens to include high-profile targets of strategic significance to China, collected by an individual or group with no political agenda *per se*. Similarly one can postulate that the targets gathered together happened less by concerted effort than by sheer coincidence. Given the groupings of various entities in the infected computer list (by country and organization), internal e-mail communications and sloppy security practices could have led to cross-infection and subsequent listing on the control servers.

Another possible explanation is that there is a single individual or set of individuals (criminal networks, for example) who are targeting these high-value targets for profit. This can be in the form of stealing financial information or critical data that can be sold to clients, be they states or private entities. There are countless examples of large-scale fraud and data theft worldwide and numerous apparent instances of outsourcing to third parties of cyber attacks and espionage, some of which the Information Warfare Monitor and its related research project, the OpenNet Initiative, have documented. *GhostNet* could very well be a for-profit, non-state venture. Even "patriotic hackers" could be acting on their own volition, or with the tacit approval of their government, as operators of the *GhostNet*.

Regardless of who or what is ultimately in control of GhostNet, its capabilities of exploitation and the strategic intelligence that can be harvested from it matter most.

Finally, it is not inconceivable that this network of infected computers could have been targeted by a state other than China, but operated physically within China (and at least one node in the United States) for strategic purposes. Compromised proxy computers on Hainan Island, for example, could have been deployed as staging posts, perhaps in an effort to deliberately mislead observers as to the true operator(s) and purpose of the *GhostNet* system.

GhostNet is significant, as it does not appear to be a typical cybercrime network. The potential political fallout is enormous. But ultimately, the question of who is behind the *GhostNet* may matter less than the strategic significance of the collection of affected targets. What this study discovered is serious evidence that information security is an item requiring urgent attention at the highest levels. It demonstrates that the subterranean layers of cyberspace, about which most users are unaware, are domains of active reconnaissance, surveillance, and exploitation.

Regardless of who or what is ultimately in control of *GhostNet*, its capabilities of exploitation and the strategic intelligence that can be harvested from it matter most. Indeed, although the Achilles' heel of the *GhostNet* system allowed us to monitor and document its far-reaching network of infiltration, we can safely hypothesize that it is neither the first nor the only one of its kind.

The United Kingdom May Be Targeted by Cyberterrorists

Imran Awan

Imran Awan is a senior lecturer in criminology at Birmingham City University in the United Kingdom. In the following viewpoint, he argues that the Internet can increasingly be used by terrorists against the United Kingdom. He says, however, that currently there is little evidence that terrorists could use the Internet to target computer systems directly. Rather, terrorists use the Internet to communicate with each other, to spread propaganda, and to spread fear or terror through videos of executions. Awan says that as terrorists' skills increase, more direct computer attacks may become commonplace.

As you read, consider the following questions:

1. In a speech before the US Congress, how did Dorothy Denning define cyberterrorism?

2. According to Awan, why is the Internet a safe haven for terrorists?

3. Who is Juba, and how does Awan say he has been used for propaganda purposes?

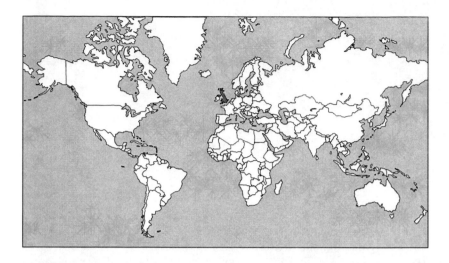

The cyber threat to Britain has intensified since recent cyber attacks from the 'Stuxnet' virus through to attacks from groups of hackers (such as LulzSec and Anonymous) who have all aimed to disrupt computer systems, and target high-profile institutions, namely Sony, the US Senate and various law enforcement agencies. Most of these cyber threats relate to criminal gangs, terrorists, hackers and hostile governments that are willing to cause cyber attacks against critical infrastructure and attack Internet systems. With 'globalisation' in an age of network systems there is a real sense of vulnerability of critical infrastructures. Moreover, this issue of cyber threats was raised and debated in 2010 by the House of Lords in Britain. Lord Reid at the time suggested that cyber threats are increasingly playing an important role as technological advances are made. His perception was that the UK [United Kingdom], like many other foreign countries, faces a realisation that cyber attacks will target critical infrastructure that have a capacity to cripple security systems (including the public and private sectors). He states that 'it is to be expected in a House like this, for all our wisdom, that we might not be as au fait with technological advances as the younger generation. However, we ignore this at our peril'. This view was reinforced by Lord Browne who in the same parliamentary debate argued that cyber threats had become more sophisticated as cyber enthusiasts begin to develop their online ambitions. He states that 'the nature and character of weaponry, is changing'.

Denning's argument is that cyber terrorism directly causes loss of life or other serious damage.

Cyber Threats

Indeed, this level of threat was further heightened by the head of the Government Communications Headquarters (GCHQ is responsible for combating cyber threats in Britain) Iain Lobban who argues that the UK is facing multifaceted cyber threats which are coming from a wide range of sources. These include worms that could disrupt governmental electronic systems. For example a hacker could interrupt runway lights or the wider electronic control at an airport by shutting down computer systems with a worm or virus. Other threats include malicious e-mails sent to government networks; cyber techniques used by countries to target different nations; the use of online theft; the threat from hackers; and finally the generic risks attached with the growth of the Internet.

According to Iain Lobban, this threat has now manifested itself to a more complex and uncertain level of terrorist threat. In a speech to the International Institute for Strategic Studies, he stated that 'Terror cyber attacks pose a real threat that goes to the heart of our economic well-being and national interest'. His assertion seems to suggest a need for a wider debate on cyber threats and also cyber terrorism. . . .

What Is Cyber Terrorism?

In the UK a terrorist is defined under s40 (1) of the Terrorism Act 2000, as a person who: (a) has committed an offence under any of sections 11, 12, 15 to 18, 54 and 56 to 63, *or* (b) is or has been concerned in the commission, preparation or instigation of acts of terrorism.

However, the term cyber terrorism has not been clearly defined with law enforcement agencies such as the FBI [Federal Bureau of Investigation] in the US and the Centre for the Protection of National Infrastructure in the UK who have all attempted to define it. Academics are also attempting to examine the potential threat of cyber terrorism: Dorothy Denning argued, in a speech given before the UK Congress, that:

> Cyber terrorism is the convergence of terrorism and cyberspace. It is generally understood to mean unlawful attacks and threats of attack against computers, networks, and the information stored therein when done to intimidate or coerce a government or its people in furtherance of political or social objectives.

Denning's argument is that cyber terrorism directly causes loss of life or other serious damage. This means the 'threat of attack on computers, networks' and attacks that could lead to 'explosions, plane crashes, water contamination or severe economic loss and even death'. This conjures up a visual picture of graphic violence, of computer technology used as a lethal weapon. She argues that attacks against critical infrastructures, such as electric power or emergency services, are possible acts of cyber terrorism.

Is Denning's description valid? Can the Internet be used to bring down an aeroplane? What is the evidence for her view? [Gabriel] Weimann for example, takes a different view. He uses the term cyber terrorism in a different sense, arguing that: 'terrorists' use of computers as a facilitator of their activities, whether for propaganda, recruitment, defaming communication or other purposes' could be forms of cyber terrorism.

To substantiate his argument, Weimann would need to show how terrorists' use of online videos and websites constitute the act of cyber terrorism. For example, are online videos of terrorist attacks a form of cyber terrorism? Or should we fear terrorists using steganography [hidden messages] which may contain hidden messages in Arabic or Urdu [the national language of Pakistan]?

Both of these views raise questions about how we define the term cyber terrorism, whether cyberspace is confined to the use of the Internet or also covers modes such as television, radio, fax, e-mail and phone calls, and so on. This [viewpoint] examines the case for both these schools of thought but concludes that the current nature of terrorism provides more support for Weimann's argument, but that this conclusion could change if terrorists acquire more sophisticated skills in new technology. . . .

Simulation Exercises: The Evidence for Cyber Terrorism?

Support for Denning's argument that computers must be used as weapons in cyber terrorism is found in the report for US Congress, 'Computer Attack and Cyberterrorism: Vulnerabilities and Policy Issues for Congress', where there were various experiments undertaken as a way of highlighting the potential threat of cyber terrorism. Part of the exercises involved the US Department of Defense (DOD) undertaking a simulation exercise that examined whether or not US ICT [information and communications technology] systems were able to protect and prevent a cyber attack. This exercise was called 'Eligible Receiver 1997' and was crucial in helping the US identify potential weaknesses they may have in the event of a cyber terrorist act.

Furthermore, another exercise called 'Eligible Receiver 2003' was used to try and play out whether the US military computer systems could cope with a cyber attack. Moreover, the Center on Terrorism and Irregular Warfare at the Naval Postgraduate School in California issued a report entitled 'Cyberterror: Prospects and Implications'. This report issued a practical simulation exercise where actors were used to examine whether or not terrorists had the skills to mount a cyber attack. Their findings seem to suggest terrorists did not have the practical skills of doing such attacks.

Part of the process included using hackers and practitioners with experience of warfare to be part of the study. The report showed that terrorists did not at the time (2002) have the sophisticated skills in information technology nor are they willing to use these tactics. However this example does also suggest that the terrorists lacked the skills to use cyber technology in the manner in which Denning predicts. Furthermore, to date, no terrorists have used cyberspace in this way. Terrorists aim to use tried and tested methods. Bringing down an aeroplane might kill innocent civilians and result in a loss of support from the community. A bomb against a legitimate target is preferable.

Cyberspace can also be used for propaganda, recruitment, training and indoctrination purposes.

Cyber Terrorism Including a Wide Spectrum of Supporting Activities

The alternative approach to Denning is Weimann's argument which is that the Internet is simply a recruitment aid, and acts as a fund-raising chat room. This form of cyber terrorism, Weimann states, '. . . can mobilise supporters to play a more active role in support of terrorist activities or causes'. Recruiters therefore may use more interactive Internet technology that they can use with online chat rooms, message boards and cybercafes, looking for enlisting support from the most naive and vulnerable and those that hold an identity crisis, namely young people.

The Internet is a safe haven for terrorists as they can remain anonymous, do not need to travel, and do not need to reveal their true identity. For example, the online terrorist

Younis Tsouli who used the name *Irhabi* (terrorist) *007* to hide his real appearance had been trained and equipped to use computers as an agent for a cyber-terrorist attack. He was instrumental in preparing al-Qaeda's online strategy and framework which consisted of propaganda campaigns, recruitment and translating al-Qaeda material from Arabic into English (this included an al-Qaeda e-book). In 2007, he was convicted in the UK for inciting terror through the use of the Internet. Academics, however, have made the point that no matter how influential cyberspace is for terrorist groups, the use of actual physical domains for terror purposes is at the forefront of extremist groups' ideological agendas. [Joshua A.] Geltzer argues that online terrorist material does not have the same impact as physical training camps have. He uses the example of the July 7/7 bombers in Britain [referring to a terrorist attack in London in 2005 that targeted the public transit system] who had less contact with online terrorist websites but instead evidence shows that they had taken part in a number of rigorous physical training sessions that required little use of computers.

Forms of Communication

Cyberspace can also be used for propaganda, recruitment, training and indoctrination purposes. The Internet also offers advantages to terrorists in that they can hide their messages. Thus, terrorists have used sophisticated encryption tools so as to deceive as highlighted in the case of one of the September 11 [2001 World Trade Center] bombers, Mohammed Atta, who was using encryption and secret coded messages via his MSN e-mail account to communicate with the other 9/11 bombers. One such tool that he used was steganography. This aims to hide information and create complex codes and in cases of cyber terrorism, this may be images, audio and text. Where the language is not one that is easily identifiable, it is easier to hide codes and more difficult for the security services to trace.

Terrorist Videos and the Press

The *Boston Phoenix* touched off a media maelstrom when it published on its website a link to a four-minute video created by the terrorists who executed *Wall Street Journal* reporter Daniel Pearl. The video showed Pearl forced to talk about his Jewish background while images of Palestinian suffering were shown on screen. Then, after a quick fade-out, Pearl's lifeless body is seen on screen as one of the executioners hacks his head off and holds it up for the camera. Pearl's father weighed in on the decision to publish this photo in an opinion piece for the *New York Times* where he pleaded with American news media "to preserve the dignity of our champions, we should remove all terrorist-produced murder scenes from our websites and agree to suppress such scenes in the future." Other journalists condemned the publication of photos or videos of Pearl's death. However, some argued that journalists who chose not to print or air the images afforded a courtesy to a fellow journalist, which would not be given to others. Further, the video was already available on websites that specialized in displaying disgusting photos. News organizations put the images in the proper context. . . .

But this defense of the photos might ignore the very real possibility that showing graphic images did not aid in the audience learning about this significant issue.

Brooke Barnett and Amy Reynolds,
Terrorism and the Press: An Uneasy Relationship.
New York: Peter Long Publishing, 2009, pp. 82–83.

In order to tackle this problem and find out what these hidden codes mean, there would need to be individuals with the appropriate language skills and insight into cryptic messages. MI6 [the British secret intelligence agency] continuously uses high-risk marketing strategies to hire people from ethnic minority communities to act as informants. This approach has been used before; for example, Special Branch recruited people from Northern Ireland in the early 1990s using the local population as informants who provided key intelligence on the Irish Republican Army (IRA). It is, however, more problematic and difficult to recruit from the Pakistani, Afghani, Yemeni and Somali communities because there is a history of mistrust between the intelligence services and Muslim communities. . . .

Cyberspace is being increasingly used for hundreds of people who are posting questions to the al-Qaeda leadership online.

Another form of propaganda is the use of online video games to train potential terrorists. This form of online video games offers real-life simulation of warlike scenarios where online gamers are able to fight in simulation exercises that are based on unpopular wars and foreign policies (such as Iraq or Afghanistan). Such games have the potential to ignite and nurture further extremism and also resentment. There is also a real possibility that online gamers will develop a violent culture and perspective through their experiences of warfare, and use it as a real-life tool for committing a terrorist attack in the future.

There have been a number of examples of where individuals have re-enacted those experiences online and wanted to re-live the experience. Furthermore, there is an intense debate in the UK (at the time of writing) with respect to the impact of computer games such as *Modern Warfare*. The game offers players the virtual sensation of fighting against either the Taliban or al-Qaeda. Critics argue that the game risks losing its moral code as it encourages the killing of individuals (based on similar scenes that resemble what happened in Mumbai [in

2008, where 164 people were killed in coordinated terror attacks]) which will only feed further extremism and antagonism. This is certainly not a passive experience and is meant to be as realistic as possible, and it is this realism which has caused so much controversy. . . .

Recruitment

Websites are a powerful tool for extremist organisations. They can secure membership without directly approaching potential recruits and the messages on websites can reach thousands of people across the world. [Abdel Bari] Atwan acknowledges that al-Qaeda has become a web-based organisation that utilizes cyberspace for terrorist purposes. Indeed, websites contain information about historical accounts, statistics and graphic imagery of terrorist material that can be downloaded and sent to millions of people. This helps create support and act as a recruitment tool. The key to such extremist ideology over the web is to create sites that cause further resentment for the West and allows international Muslim support by allowing its audience to reach to millions. Therefore websites are now being used by a wide range of terrorist groups who understand that a website is key to having a global reach. Furthermore, one of the core issues with terrorist websites is the potential to recruit innocent people who may have felt compromised and been allured by what they have seen online and thus become radicalised. . . .

Furthermore, one of al-Qaeda's media arms (known as 'As-Sahab', which is Arabic for 'the clouds') has had a leading role in recruitment of a wide audience. According to Intel-Center, who monitors al-Qaeda's media operations, they argue that *As-Sahab* releases around 58 videos every day. Indeed, cyberspace is being increasingly used for hundreds of people who are posting questions to the al-Qaeda leadership online. This view is reinforced by SITE [Search for International Terrorist Entities] in Washington, which described a question and answer session with al-Qaeda's Ayman al-Zawahiri, as deeply 'disturbing'. Moreover, *As-Sahab* produced a further 90 videos in the year 2007. These videos of Osama bin Laden and Ayman al-Zawahiri act as propaganda tools and aim to use information technology as a way for al-Qaeda to reach a global audience.

> *Live executions ... have become part of the cyber terrorist act. ... The aim is not only to cause fear but also to humiliate and demonstrate power.*

Communication and Propaganda

Al-Qaeda are now using the Internet to promote and indoctrinate their audience by propaganda means through videotapes of its leaders condemning the West, selling T-shirts, flags and pictures of senior al-Qaeda figures, CD-ROMs, DVDs and photographs, all of the merchandise above acts as recruitment messages and advertises the al-Qaeda brand globally. For example videotapes of the Baghdad sniper Juba are readily available on the Internet and are used by al-Qaeda to show how foreign policy in Iraq has failed [after the American invasion in 2003].

These videos show Juba killing American soldiers in Iraq without actually showing his face but show Juba as an immortalised figure and depicted as a freedom fighter. Some of the videos are available on the Internet with the aim of this propaganda to disseminate information through various online terrorist means. These videos, however, are seen in some communities as a justification for suicide attacks. The key aim of this propaganda is to disseminate information through various online terrorist means. ...

A Tool of Terror

Whether the Internet is a tool of terror continues to be unclear. Some extremist organisations have used websites to show live online killing of Western hostages. This began with Nick Berg's and then Ken Bigley's and Daniel Pearl's killings.[1] Since then there have been further cases of such executions with many British hostages being held as ransom in an attempt to persuade the UK to change its foreign policy. Using the Internet and videos to make such demands has changed the way information technology can be used.

Geltzer argues that both websites and chat rooms may provide grounds for al-Qaeda to disseminate literature globally but that the central issue is not being tackled—that is, how are websites or chat rooms linked to actual al-Qaeda terrorist acts? Furthermore, he argues, that all that the Internet has done is too bring al-Qaeda together to communicate more quickly but that these communications do not produce actual terrorist atrocities. Live executions, for example transmitted to a global audience, have become part of the cyber terrorist act, as it appears to be the direct link between the use of the Internet and a direct terrorist act. The aim is not only to cause fear but also to humiliate and demonstrate power. As a result terrorist groups continue to broadcast these videos online.

Moreover the aim is not to create support or recruitment but to strike fear into the hearts and minds of people. These are the same hearts and minds that the former British prime minister Gordon Brown had stated needed to be won. The case of Edwin Dyer, a British hostage killed by al-Qaeda in July 2009, highlights how al-Qaeda now are using online videos to make demands against countries. In this case, the demand was for the release of Abu Qatada, a senior al-Qaeda figure. The message which was posted by the group Al-Qaeda in the Islamic Maghreb (AQIM) stated that 'we demand that Britain release Sheikh Abu Qatada, who is unjustly [held], for the release of its British citizen. We give it 20 days as of the is-

---

1. Nick Berg was an American businessman killed in 2004; Ken Bigley was an English civil engineer killed in 2004; and Daniel Pearl was an American journalist killed in 2002.

suance of this statement. . . . When this period expires, the Mujahideen [Islamic fighters] will kill the British hostage'.

Furthermore, critics argue it does not matter whether al-Qaeda uses a fax or a telephone call, any form of communication can still form part of the cyber terrorist act. Therefore no matter whether it is the Internet, websites, chat rooms, e-mail, telephone or fax, it remains a form of communication used by al-Qaeda which is part of the cyber terrorist attack as demonstrated in the Mumbai bombings where the suspects used mobile phones in order to directly communicate with terrorist leaders in Pakistan who gave the orders on the killing of innocent people.

Denning vs. Weimann

Denning and Weimann have both argued that cyber terrorism is a real threat. The Denning argument has always placed the threat on the use of computers to destroy critical infrastructure, such as financial, military and governmental sectors. Conversely, the Weimann argument is that terrorists use the Internet as a means of propaganda and recruitment. . . .

Recruitment, propaganda and raising funds can now all be done online through websites. The UK, like the US, has implemented new policies in this matter and further changes can be expected in the near future as the threat of cyber terrorism becomes more noticeable. Therefore, the current nature of terrorism provides more support for Weimann's argument but this view could change if terrorists become more sophisticated in their skills.

Periodical and Internet Sources Bibliography

The following articles have been selected to supplement the diverse views presented in this chapter.

Nate Anderson	"Confirmed: US and Israel Created Stuxnet, Lost Control of It," Ars Technica, June 1, 2012. http://arstechnica.com.
Jack Cloherty	"Virtual Terrorism: Al Qaeda Video Calls for 'Electronic Jihad,'" ABC News, May 22, 2012.
Economist	"The Threat from the Internet: Cyberwar," July 1, 2010.
Richard Esposito	"'Astonishing' Cyber Espionage Threat from Foreign Governments: British Spy Chief," ABC News, June 25, 2012.
Tom Gjelten	"U.S. Not Afraid to Say It: China's the Cyber Bad Guy," NPR, February 18, 2012.
Ellen Nakashima and Joby Warrick	"Stuxnet Was Work of U.S. and Israeli Experts, Officials Say," *Washington Post*, June 1, 2012.
NPR	"China's Cyber Threat a High-Stakes Spy Game," November 27, 2011.
Paul Taylor	"New Cyber Spying Virus Found in Lebanon," *Financial Times*, August 9, 2012.
Pete Warren	"State-Sponsored Cyber Espionage Projects Now Prevalent, Say Experts," *Guardian*, August 30, 2012.
Christopher Williams	"Cyber Espionage Virus Targets Lebanese Banks," *Telegraph*, August 10, 2012.

For Further Discussion

Chapter 1

1. Which is more responsible for cybercrime vulnerability: cultural factors or technological factors? Explain your answer using evidence from the viewpoints in this chapter.

2. If you were the manager of a bank, would you purchase insurance against cybercrime? Why or why not? Based on the viewpoint by John Greenwood, what factors would influence your decision?

Chapter 2

1. Based on the viewpoints by Lynette Lee Corporal, Stefan Simons, and Human Rights Watch, which seems most restrictive, the cybercrime law of Thailand, France, or Iraq? Explain your reasoning.

2. Based on the viewpoints in this chapter, is it better to target cybercrime using specifically crafted cybercrime laws or using already existing laws and institutions? Explain your reasoning.

Chapter 3

1. Based on the viewpoints in this chapter, are cybercriminals most dangerous when they are highly skilled hackers? Explain your answer.

Chapter 4

1. Based on the viewpoints in this chapter, which nations are the most likely to perpetrate cyber espionage? Explain your answer.

2. Based on the viewpoint by Imran Awan, what is the greatest danger posed by cyberterrorism? Explain your answer.

Organizations to Contact

The editors have compiled the following list of organizations concerned with the issues debated in this book. The descriptions are derived from materials provided by the organizations. All have publications or information available for interested readers. The list was compiled on the date of publication of the present volume; the information provided here may change. Be aware that many organizations take several weeks or longer to respond to inquiries, so allow as much time as possible.

Berkman Center for Internet & Society
23 Everett Street, 2nd Floor, Cambridge, MA   02138
(617) 495-7547 • fax: (617) 495-7641
e-mail: cyber@law.harvard.edu
website: http://cyber.law.harvard.edu

The Berkman Center for Internet & Society conducts research on legal, technical, and social developments in cyberspace and assesses the need or lack thereof for laws and sanctions. It publishes a monthly newsletter—the *Filter*—blog posts, and articles based on the center's research efforts, many of which are available on its website, including the final report of the Internet Safety Technical Task Force, "Enhancing Child Safety & Online Technologies."

Bureau of Justice Statistics (BJS)
810 Seventh Street NW, Washington, DC   20531
(202) 307-0765
e-mail: askbjs@usdoj.gov
website: www.ojp.usdoj.gov/bjs

The mission of the Bureau of Justice Statistics (BJS), an agency of the US Department of Justice, is to collect, analyze, publish, and disseminate information on crime, criminal offenders, victims of crime, and the operation of justice systems at all levels of government. These data are critical to US federal, state, and local policy makers in combating crime and ensuring that justice is both efficient and evenhanded. BJS's website offers a clearinghouse of statistics from all areas of criminal justice.

Cato Institute

1000 Massachusetts Avenue NW
Washington, DC 20001-5403
(202) 842-0200 • fax: (202) 842-3490
e-mail: cato@cato.org
website: www.cato.org

The Cato Institute is a libertarian public policy research foundation. It evaluates government policies and offers reform proposals. Topics of its policy analyses include "From Cybercrime Statistics to Cyberspying" and "Electronic Pearl Harbor?: More Hype than Threat." In addition, the institute publishes the bimonthly newsletter *Cato Policy Report* and the triannual *Cato Journal*.

Computer Crime Research Center (CCRC)

Box 8010, Zaporozhye 95 69095
 Ukraine
website: www.crime-research.org

The Computer Crime Research Center (CCRC) is a nonprofit, nongovernmental scientific research organization that conducts research in legal, criminal, and criminological problems of cybercrime. Based in Ukraine, its English website contains many articles about cybercrime as well as news and links.

Cybercrime Law

website: www.cybercrimelaw.net

Cybercrime Law is a global information clearinghouse on cybercrime law containing a comprehensive survey of current legislation from around the world that includes the laws of seventy-eight countries, plus news about cybercrime from around the world.

Electronic Frontier Foundation (EFF)

454 Shotwell Street, San Francisco, CA   94110-1914
(415) 436-9333 • fax: (415) 436-9993
website: www.eff.org

The Electronic Frontier Foundation (EFF) is the leading civil liberties group defending the rights of the public in the digital world. Its website contains numerous articles and posts, including "Protecting Privacy in Uruguay and Across the Globe" and "Google Under Pressure from EU Regulators on Privacy Policy."

Global Internet Freedom Consortium

e-mail: contact@internetfreedom.org
website: www.internetfreedom.com

The Global Internet Freedom Consortium is made up of organizations that develop and deploy anticensorship technologies for use by Internet users in countries whose governments restrict web-based information access. It particularly focuses on Internet freedom in China. Its website includes information about its activities, white papers, and research reports such as "Battle for Freedom in Chinese Cyberspace" and "Report on Google.cn's Self-Censorship."

Human Rights Watch

350 Fifth Avenue, 34th floor, New York, NY   10118-3299
(212) 290-4700 • fax: (212) 736-1300
e-mail: hrwnyc@hrw.org
website: www.hrw.org

Founded in 1978, Human Rights Watch is a nongovernmental organization that conducts systematic investigations of human rights abuses in countries around the world. It publishes many books, reports, and articles on specific countries and issues relating to human rights violations. Its website includes numerous discussions of human rights and Internet issues, including "Vietnam: Stop Cyber Attacks Against Online Critics" and "Russia: Internet Legislation Merits Greater Scrutiny Before Passage."

**Internet Services Providers' Association,
United Kingdom (ISPA UK)**
1 Castle Lane, London   SW1E 6DR
   United Kingdom
020 3397 3304 • fax: 0871 594 0298
e-mail: admin@ispa.org.uk
website: www.ispa.org.uk

The mission of the Internet Services Providers' Association,
United Kingdom (ISPA UK) is to provide essential support for
Internet services and promote collaboration between its members and the wider Internet community. It advocates before
government bodies on behalf of the Internet industry and users. It publishes *Political Monitor*, a weekly newsletter for
members that focuses on political issues affecting the Internet
industry. Its website also includes press releases and information about events and policies.

i-SAFE Inc.
6189 El Camino Real, Suite 201, Carlsbad, CA   92009
(760) 603-7911 • fax: (760) 603-8382
website: www.isafe.org

i-SAFE Inc. is a nonprofit foundation dedicated to teaching
students how to use the Internet safely, responsibly, and pro-
ductively, as well as how to avoid inappropriate and unlawful
online content. It publishes online learning programs and
provides educational services such as the i-LEARN online program and the iMentor network.

Bibliography of Books

Mark Bowden   *Worm: The First Digital World War.*
                       New York: Atlantic Monthly Press,
                       2011.

Susan W. Brenner *Cyberthreats: The Emerging Fault
                  Lines of the Nation State.* New York:
                  Oxford University Press, 2009.

Roderic   *Cyber-Crime: The Challenge in Asia.*
Broadhurst and   Hong Kong: Hong Kong University
Peter Grabosky,   Press, 2005.
eds.

Jeffrey Carr   *Inside Cyber Warfare: Mapping the
                       Cyber Underworld.* Sebastopol, CA:
                       O'Reilley Media, 2010.

Clare   *Virtual Economies and Financial
Chambers-Jones   Crime: Money Laundering in Cyber-
                       space.* Northampton, MA: Edward
                       Elgar, 2012.

Richard A. Clarke *Cyber War: The Next Threat to Na-
and Robert K.   tional Security and What to Do About
Knake   It.* New York: Ecco, 2012.

Misha Glenny   *DarkMarket: Cyberthieves, Cybercops,
                       and You.* New York: Alfred A. Knopf,
                       2011.

Debarati Halder   *Cyber Crime and the Victimization of
and K. Jaishankar Women: Laws, Rights and Regulations.*
                   Hershey, PA: Information Science
                   Reference, 2012.

K. Jaishankar	*Cyber Criminology: Exploring Internet Crimes and Criminal Behavior*. Boca Raton, FL: CRC Press, 2011.
Yvonne Jewkes and Majid Yar, eds.	*Handbook of Internet Crime*. Devon, UK: Willan Publishing, 2010.
Robert K. Knake	*Internet Governance in an Age of Cyber Insecurity*. New York: Council on Foreign Relations, 2010.
Franklin D. Kramer, Stuart H. Starr, and Larry K. Wentz, eds.	*Cyberpower and National Security*. Washington, DC: National Defense University Press, 2009.
Rebecca MacKinnon	*Consent of the Networked: The Worldwide Struggle for Internet Freedom*. New York: Basic Books, 2012.
Joseph Menn	*Fatal System Error: The Hunt for the New Crime Lords Who Are Bringing Down the Internet*. New York: PublicAffairs, 2010.
Evgeny Morozov	*The Net Delusion: The Dark Side of Internet Freedom*. New York: PublicAffairs, 2011.
Kevin Poulsen	*Kingpin: How One Hacker Took Over the Billion-Dollar Cybercrime Underground*. New York: Crown Publishers, 2011.
Christian Schwarzenegger and Sarah Summers	*The Emergence of EU Criminal Law: Cyber Crime and the Regulation of the Information Society*. Oxford, UK: Hart Publishing, 2013.

Zeinab Karake Shalhoub and Sheikha Lubna Al Qasimi — *Cyber Law and Cyber Security in Developing and Emerging Economies.* Northampton, MA: Edward Elgar, 2010.

Russell G. Smith, Peter N. Grabosky, and Gregor F. Urbas — *Cyber Criminals on Trial.* New York: Cambridge University Press, 2004.

Abraham D. Sofaer and Seymour E. Goodman, eds. — *The Transnational Dimension of Cyber Crime and Terrorism.* Stanford, CA: Hoover Institution Press, 2001.

Russell Southwood — *Less Walk, More Talk: How Celtel and the Mobile Phone Changed Africa.* Hoboken, NJ: Wiley, 2009.

Nicole S. van der Meulen — *Financial Identity Theft: Context, Challenges and Countermeasures.* The Hague, Netherlands: T.M.C. Asser Press, 2011.

David Wise — *Tiger Trap: America's Secret Spy War with China.* New York: Houghton Mifflin Harcourt, 2011.

Index

Geographic headings and page numbers in **boldface** refer to viewpoints about that country or region.

CPSIA information can be obtained
at www.ICGtesting.com
Printed in the USA
FFOW02n1649260913